Elevating Student Voice

Elevating Student Voice

How to Enhance Student Participation, Citizenship and Leadership

Nelson Beaudoin

EYE ON EDUCATION
6 Depot Way West, Suite 106
Larchmont, N.Y. 10538

Library of Congress Cataloging-in-Publication Data

Beaudoin, Nelson.
  Elevating student voice: how to enhance student participation, citizenship and
leadership / Nelson Beaudoin.
    p. cm.
  Includes bibliographical references.
  ISBN-13: 978-1-59667-015-0
  ISBN-10: 1-59667-015-0
1. High school students—United States. 2. Citizenship—Study and teaching
(Secondary)—United States. 3. Educational leadership—United States. I. Title.
  LA229.B355 2005
  371.18—dc22

                                2005025190

Production services:
UB Communications
10 Lodge Lane
Parsippany, NJ 07054
973.331.9391

Also available from Eye On Education

**Stepping Outside Your Comfort Zone:
Lessons for School Leaders**
Nelson Beaudoin

What Great Principals Do *Differently:*
15 Things That Matter Most
Todd Whitaker

**What Successful Principals Do!
169 Tips for Principals**
Franzy Fleck

BRAVO Principal!
Sandra Harris

**The Administrator's Guide to
School Community Relations, Second Edition**
George E. Pawlas

Talk It Out!
The Educator's Guide to Successful Difficult Conversations
Barbara E. Sanderson

**Making the Right Decisions:
A Guide for School Leaders**
Douglas J. Fiore and Chip Joseph

Dealing with Difficult Teachers, Second Edition
Todd Whitaker

**Dealing with Difficult Parents
(And with Parents in Difficult Situations)**
Todd Whitaker and Douglas Fiore

Great Quotes for Great Educators
Todd Whitaker and Dale Lumpa

**School Leader Internship: Developing, Monitoring,
and Evaluating Your Leadership Experience, 2nd Ed.**
Martin, Wright, Danzig, Flanary, and Brown

What Great Teachers Do *Differently:*
14 Things That Matter Most
Todd Whitaker

20 Strategies for
Collaborative School Leaders
Jane Clark Lindle

Motivating and Inspiring Teachers:
The Educational Leader's Guide for Building Staff Morale
Todd Whitaker, Beth Whitaker, and Dale Lumpa

The Principal as Instructional Leader:
A Handbook for Supervisors
Sally J. Zepeda

Instructional Leadership for School Improvement
Sally J. Zepeda

Six Types of Teachers: Recruiting, Retaining, and
Mentoring the Best
Douglas J. Fiore and Todd Whitaker

Supervision Across the Content Areas
Sally J. Zepeda and R. Stewart Mayers

The ISLLC Standards in Action:
A Principal's Handbook
Carol Engler

Harnessing the Power of Resistance:
A Guide for Educators
Jared Scherz

101 Answers for New Teachers and Their Mentors:
Effective Teaching Tips for Daily Classroom Use
Annette L. Breaux

Data Analysis for Continuous School Improvement
Victoria L. Bernhardt

Handbook on Teacher Evaluation:
Assessing and Improving Performance
James Stronge and Pamela Tucker

Dedication

To the thousands of students I have worked
with over the years, whose voices have inspired me—
those I have known well,
and those I wish I had known better.

Meet the Author

With over 34 years of experiences in educational leadership, Nelson Beaudoin brings practical and exciting ideas to the discussion on school reform. His work is guided by the belief that leaders should listen more than talk, care more than judge, and understand more than guess.

Beaudoin has led two high schools through a Comprehensive School Reform grant. His schools have received national recognition both as a Service Learning Leader School (2001) and as a First Amendment School (2004). He was selected as Maine's 2000 NASSP Principal of the Year.

He has presented his message about inspirational leadership, the magic of student voice, and creating a culture of change to audiences throughout the country. His faculty's work on professional learning communities, student-led conferences and student engagement has been replicated in a number of schools.

His first book, *Stepping Outside Your Comfort Zone: Lessons for School Leaders*, demonstrates that great things can happen when school leaders refuse to settle for business as usual.

Nelson Beaudoin is currently principal at Kennebunk High School in Kennebunk, Maine.

Table of Contents

Dedication   vii

Meet the Author   ix

INTRODUCTION: THE MAGIC OF
STUDENT VOICE   1

1. CHANGING THE VIEW   5
   Getting Students to Care   5
   A School for Each Kid   7
   A Sense of Belonging   9
   Students as Possibilities   13
   Inspiration versus Control   15
   Prisoners or Volunteers   18

2 CHANGING THE PRACTICE   21
   Step Outside the Comfort Zone   21
   The Leader Sets the Tone   22
   Choose Your Attitude   23
   No Secrecy, No Surprises   25
   The Earlier, the Better   26
   It's Not about the Recipe   27
   Commit to the Journey   29

3 PAYING HEED TO STUDENT VOICE   31
   It's All about Choices   31
   The Survey Says   33
   Advisory: Students Speak, We Listen   34
   An Open Door   36
   Let's Talk about It Together   37
   Advisors and the School Also Benefit   38
   Student-Led Conferences   38

Student Feedback to Teachers 42
    Sample Course Feedback Form 44
Student Speakers 46

4   LINKING CLASSROOM AND COMMUNITY . . . 49
Community Service 49
Service Learning 51
    The Greatest Generation Project 52
    Family Treasures 52
    Teaching Foreign Language 52
    Wetland Mitigation 53
    Jump Rope for Heart 53
    Tree Hugger and Friends 54
    Modern-Day Slavery 54
    Middle School Gender Project 54
Student-Directed Programs and Events 55
Experiential Learning 57

5   SHOWCASING TALENTS, BUILDING SKILLS . . 61
Spotlight on Students 63
Special Student Clubs 64
    Peer Mediators 64
    Civil Rights Team 65
    D.A.R.T. Team 66
    KHS Connections 67
    Peer Helpers 68
    And many more 69
Student Publications 69
    Newspaper Guidelines: 2004–2005 71
    Ramblings Point Sheets: 2004–2005 72

6   EDUCATING FOR CITIZENSHIP 81
Citizenship Matters 81
Educating for Democracy 82
The Civic Mission of Schools 83
Student Governance 84

Students on Committees 87
Student Interviewers 88
Student Representation on the School Board . . . 90
Student Board Members 90
Kennebunk High School: Student Board
Members Selection Procedures 92
Draft—Student Board Member Application
for the Class of 2005 93
Levels of Responsibility 93
Maine School Administrative District 71
Code of Conduct 94
A Mission-Driven School 96
Mission Statement 96

7 HIGHLIGHTING THE FIRST AMENDMENT . . . 99
A Second-Rate Issue? 99
Educating for Freedom and Responsibility 100
First Amendment Schools: Vision Statement . . 102
Core Civic Habits Practiced in First
Amendment Schools 106

8 FINDING INSPIRATION FOR THE JOURNEY . . 109
Barnstable: Service Learning on Cape Cod 109
Mark Grashow: A Mosquito in Brooklyn 112
Federal Hocking High School:
A Laboratory of Democracy 114
Quest High School: A Texas Dynamo 115
Lanier High School: Aiming High in Jackson . . 119
Ten Ways Parents Can Reinforce First
Ammendment Principles at Home 120
Butler Middle School: A Civic-Minded
Middle School 122
Snapshots 124

CONCLUSION: CLOSING THE CIRCLE 127

BIBLIOGRAPHY 129

Introduction: The Magic of Student Voice

I believe in the magic of student voice. Honoring student voice is an essential part of great schooling. Yet the literature contains very little on student voice in contemporary schools. Sadly, what should be a reality in American education is instead a rarity.

I have come to trust student voice as a powerful tool for school improvement, a liberating force for student engagement, and a crucial element in educating for participatory democracy. I have written this book to convey the magic of student voice to all who value these goals.

A recent exploration on the Internet took me to an article that talked of professional educators ignoring student voice "to the extent that it is considered to be immature, frivolous or ephemeral."[1] In my experience, student voice is rarely any of these.

True, students themselves may be immature. But they come to school as they are, and professional educators need to listen to them if we value their participation and engagement in school. In these pages, readers will discover ways to develop student voice—indeed, a fairly organized, established protocol for doing so—and find story after story of how students respond when we heed their voices.

Nor do I consider student voice a frivolous matter. I take educating for citizenship seriously. In order for our country's experiment in democracy to endure, educators must allow students to practice the necessary skills. Dennis Littky[2] writes that

---

[1] Edward G. Rozycki, *Cloning Student Voice*, 1999. Accessed July 28, 2005 at http://home.comcast.net/~erozycki/StudentVoice.html.
[2] Dennis Littky, *The Big Picture: Education Is Everyone's Business*, 2004.

in many cases, students go through twelve years of schooling without making one democracy-inspired decision. Shame on us! I hope that this book will help schools promote citizenship and become laboratories of democracy.

Finally, in my experience student voice is far from ephemeral. Rather, it has constituted the underpinning of schools where I have worked. Schools that promote student voice reap benefits not only for individual students, but for school climate and public relations as well. There is no better engine to pull the train of school reform than student voice, and once it picks up steam it is difficult to derail—a fact that will be unmistakable as this work unfolds.

How can educators find and use the magic of student voice? First of all, we may need to make some adjustments in how we think about school and about students. In the first chapter of this book, Changing the View, I explore the beliefs and attitudes that best support student voice. In the next, Changing the Practice, I encourage school leaders to embrace these beliefs and attitudes, and I suggest a number of leadership practices that promote student voice.

Chapter 3, Paying Heed to Student Voice, brings to the forefront the strategies, programs, and procedures that promote student voice within the formal structure of the school day. Where can students speak to their teachers and to other adults in school? What happens when we pay heed?

In Chapter 4, Linking Classroom and Community, I offer vivid examples and detailed descriptions of student voice in action. Through community service, student-directed events, service learning and experiential learning, students explore their power to make a difference in their own education and the wider community. Chapter 5 brings us back to the school grounds for a look at the extra- and co-curricular activities that showcase our students' talents, build their skills, and tap into the growing strength of their voices.

Chapter 6, Educating for Citizenship, turns to the powerful role of schools in creating opportunities for students to practice democracy and civic responsibility. Chapter 7 highlights First Amendment Schools: Educating for Freedom and Responsibility, a national reform initiative that supports schools seeking to model and apply democratic principles.

Finally, Chapter 8, Finding Inspiration for the Journey, provides examples of student voice and participatory democracy from schools across the nation. These snapshots of existing practice offer a glimpse of the many and varied ways in which school communities can embrace student voice.

I hope readers of this book will come away with a new perspective on student voice and its potential for enhancing student engagement and leadership in our schools. I hope teachers and administrators will recognize how readily they can adapt current practices and procedures to incorporate student voice in daily routines and in school improvement efforts. I trust that readers will be convinced of the indispensable need to teach and practice democracy in our schools. Finally, I predict that student voice can work magic wherever school leaders have the courage to pursue it.

1

Changing the View

Getting Students to Care

Even if we were to disregard all the research that identifies how students learn, all the programs that promote learning, and all the beliefs that support it, we would be left with one compelling reason to embrace student voice, and that is the difference it makes to students. By elevating student voice to its rightful status, we can change the way students view their learning, themselves, and their school. This change sends out ever-widening ripples. By listening to student voices, we can motivate and engage students in today's schools, and that engagement can lead to greater achievement. High levels of student engagement open the door to improved pedagogy, program innovations, and reform initiatives.

The problems of disenfranchised youth in America's schools go far beyond the factors—such as teacher shortcomings, poor facilities, inadequate funding, low test scores, societal issues, and lack of accountability—that usually get top billing from critics of our educational system. Those critics who do address low levels of student engagement link it to other factors, only rarely considering student engagement in its own right. By contrast, I view student engagement as the linchpin of great schooling. Unless we engage our students—unless we get them to care—not much else will matter.

Greeting students on the first day of school, I exchanged pleasantries with a returning senior I'll call Tim.

"How was your summer?" I asked.
"Not long enough," he answered.
"They never are, but it's good to see you again."

As I began to walk away, Tim stopped me. "You know, I was thinking about you the other day," he said.

Somewhat intrigued, I asked how in the world I had entered his thoughts during summer vacation. Tim explained that he had thought about how hard I worked at making the school better, by giving students freedom and encouraging them to act responsibly. Smiling in appreciation, I started to walk on. Tim's next words stopped me in my tracks.

"But in a way, I feel bad for you," he said.
"What do you mean?" I inquired.
"Well, I feel bad because, you know, some of our students just don't care! You do all this work and some people just don't care!"

My response was swift and instinctive. "Oh, thanks so much for thinking of me, but don't be concerned. I realize that some students don't care. But I can tell you that ten percent more care than cared the year before, which was ten percent more than the year before that. I know I can't possibly get everyone to care, but as long as the numbers are going in the right direction, I intend to keep doing what I am doing."

My response was based on survey data about Kennebunk High School students' enthusiasm for learning, collected over the previous four years. As Figure 1 illustrates, the data show a dramatic increase in positive student responses to the question, "Does this school make you enthusiastic about learning?" I attribute that increase to attitudes, practices, and programs that improved student engagement by promoting student voice. We can change the view. We can get kids to care!

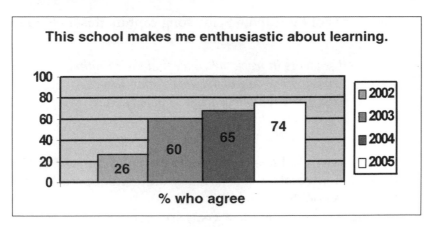

Figure 1

A School for Each Kid

Many years ago, an ad campaign for McDonald's restaurant chain used the slogan *"We do it all for you!"* to suggest that customers needn't worry about decisions when ordering food: *"Two all-beef patties, special sauce, lettuce, cheese, pickles, onions, on a sesame seed bun!"* In contrast, the Burger King franchises chose a different approach: *"Hold the pickles, hold the lettuce, special orders don't upset us!"* Burger King's slogan was *"Have it your way."*

I'm not going to make judgments about fast-food restaurants—but if the slogan "We do it all for you!" described a school, I think it would be a "school for all kids," where all students take practically the same program involving core subjects in a very traditional setting. At a school that says, "Have it your way," students would participate in a variety of personalized programs that honor their strengths and interests. This is a "school for each kid"—and I support this approach. Rather than trying to get all kids to fit the same structure, I want each student to find a structure that fits. Rather than having individual students following predictable courses of study, I want them to pursue passions leading to adventurous learning. I don't view students as spectators who let education happen to them. School is about students, and their participation is nonnegotiable.

The words of this Monte Selby song capture this idea quite well:

"All students in reach, when we find their rhythm
The step, the dance, the song within them.
That's a better journey, but so much harder.
Too extraordinary, but so much smarter.
To drum to the beat of each different marcher."

Most schools would have all students march to the beat of the same drum. I advocate a substantially different approach—developing "a school for each kid."

During a state review last year, six parents were asked to identify the most impressive outcome of their child's education at Kennebunk High School. In different words, each parent gave essentially the same response: "Our daughter [or son] learned self-advocacy skills." It stands to reason that self-advocacy is more likely to occur in "a school for each kid."

After the 2004 commencement, I received the following note from a graduating senior:

Mr. Beaudoin,

I can't thank you enough for the countless opportunities and support you gave me this past year. Between tutoring in the writing lab and speaking at the school board meetings, <u>I truly feel that I have left a lasting impression on KHS</u>. I could not have done that without you. Kennebunk High School is extremely fortunate to have you.

Thank you again and I will keep in touch.

Fondly,

Eileen

In a departure from the typical thank-you note, this student writes of her contribution to the school. A school that works to personalize programming for each student, to accent their strengths and interests, sets the stage for students to feel a strong sense of accomplishment. Rather than looking at school solely from the standpoint of what it did for her, Eileen was able to look at what she contributed. John F. Kennedy understood that a volunteer spirit would advance citizenship: "Ask not what your country can do for you; ask what you can do for your country." We will return to this idea of service as an important aspect of "a school for each kid."

A Sense of Belonging

The National Center for Student Aspirations[3] works to help students live up to their greatest potential. The Center's work has identified eight conditions that create optimum chances for success. Reading between the lines of Eileen's brief note, we find the three foundational conditions: belonging, heroes, and a sense of accomplishment.

Eileen's note definitely gives the impression that she belonged in our school community. Students who have this sense of belonging rarely miss school; they know their absence would be noticed. The fact that Eileen tutored in the writing lab meant that other students depended on her for academic support. She was also a drama student, and the production company would have suffered had she missed school.

Eileen had heroes—adults she could look up to, who listened to what she had to say. As the student council's historian, Eileen had the responsibility of reporting student council activities at monthly school board meetings. School board members, drama coaches, teachers, administrators, and parents were important to Eileen, and they all showed a willingness to listen to her.

The final foundational condition speaks about students having a sense of accomplishment. Clearly, Eileen believes she has made a difference in her school community. She undoubtedly saw her time in high school through a lens of giving, rather than a lens of receiving.

---

[3] See http:www.studentaspiration.org/index.asp, accessed July 28, 2005.

The National Center for Student Aspirations also lists three motivational conditions: fun and excitement, curiosity and creativity, and a spirit of adventure. As we investigate ways to get students more engaged in their school and their learning, these motivational conditions will come into play. So much of the incentive for learning is found in these conditions, and student voice can have a dramatic effect in advancing them.

The Center rounds out its list of conditions underpinning student success with two that imply a lifelong mindset of aspirations: leadership and responsibility, and the confidence to take action. These too will surface throughout this work, particularly when we address civic responsibility and democratic practices. The idea that students should be given opportunities to lead, to make decisions, and to experience the consequences is really about creating citizenship skills.

Eileen's words support the major theme of this chapter: Schools that set out to create "a school for each kid" can engender a sense of belonging in their students more readily than schools that treat all students the same. Schools can promote this sense of belonging in many ways, from simply caring about the students personally to providing special activities that honor students' strengths and interests.

Choosing a reluctant learner as the "keeper" of the classroom pencils offers a simple example of giving students a sense of purpose. Teachers who assign classroom duties contribute to a sense of belonging in their students. When done thoughtfully, constructing classroom chores can have a positive effect on learning outcomes and student accountability. All students can grow from these experiences that promote individual value and teach responsibility.

School clubs and organizations foster the sense of belonging that is so critical for young people. While budget discussions often sideline athletic teams, art programs, and school clubs as dispensable, they provide strong opportunities for drawing students in. Many students identify with the teams, clubs or activities they join. These co-curricular and extracurricular pursuits give students a reason to come to school.

Kennebunk High School, a school of 850 students, offers other examples of how students build a sense of belonging. Every

Wednesday, the class day at KHS starts 90 minutes later than usual so teachers can work collaboratively to improve teaching practices and school programs. Most of the students love the opportunity to sleep in, but a significant number (approximately 15 percent) come to school at the regular time.

Some of these students have a special group or activity they don't want to miss, such as Writers Club, Captains Club or Chess Club. But many of the early morning crowd come to school simply because they feel comfortable there. For some, home is not all it should be. Others come to be with their friends; young people need to socialize. Regardless of the reason, I'm glad to see students wanting to come to school. They belong here!

Students also demonstrate this sense of belonging at Kennebunk High School during the 45 minutes after the first bus arrives. Before the start of the class day, students are free to go anywhere in the building in a peripherally supervised situation (a few adults are on duty in general areas). What we see during this time on a typical day highlights the concept of belonging.

In the upstairs hallway near the elevator, ten sophomores sit on the floor. Four of them are playing a battery-operated game—a game designed for younger children, but these fifteen-year-olds are having a blast. The same group gathers here daily, mostly to study and hang out with friends. If any one were absent, the other nine would notice.

Another swarm of about 30 "regulars"—a real cross section of KHS students—starts the day down the hall in Mr. J's room. Some are playing chess, others a complex fantasy card game, still others a spirited round of Battleship. A few are simply talking about the weekend's NASCAR race. Mr. J is playing in one of the card games. Whether he knows it or not, he is providing these students with a home base, a place of belonging that boosts their enjoyment of school.

Similar gatherings form throughout the building—some because of a special bond with a teacher, others because of a particular interest in sports, or shared academic curiosity, or a social relationship. It's not a bunch of cliques; the point is that students have the freedom to roam, to make themselves comfortable. The time honors who they are and encourages their sense of belonging.

Teenagers have a monumental need to fit in, a fundamental need to belong. Schools can help them meet this need simply by acknowledging its importance. Furthermore, I believe that for a school to succeed, its students must have a sense of belonging at school. A great many of the other topics explored in this book contribute to this important idea.

Bonnie Benard[4] is a strong national voice in the work around resiliency in the fields of prevention and education. In her research on the benefits of environmental protective factors to student success, she cites three factors that have held up under scrutiny: caring relationships, high expectations, and opportunities to participate and contribute. These ideas resonate throughout this section on the value of promoting a sense of belonging for our students.

When we present students with opportunities to be involved in school improvement work, when we give them a say in the decisions that affect them, we increase their sense of belonging and accomplishment. At Kennebunk High School, we have tracked student perceptions of the impact of student voice on the school. The survey data, collected over a four-year period, are graphed in Figure 2. The results show a steady increase in

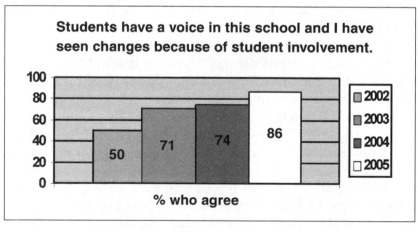

Figure 2

---

[4] Bonnie Benard, *Resiliency: What We Have Learned*, 2004.

student voice and school change. I'm convinced that this has led to a greater sense of belonging in our students.

Students as Possibilities

The adage that we spend 95 percent of our time and energy on 5 percent of our students tells a lot about how schools function. A certain few students challenge us with their inappropriate choices and behaviors. The amount of attention we devote to this small segment of our student population sets us up to look at students as problems rather than possibilities.

Those in our schools and communities who do recognize the possibilities students offer often seem to imply that only some of our young people fit into this category. High school students, in particular, tend to draw criticism as they spread their wings and learn to fly. It's all too easy for adults to categorize, judge, and constrain.

I recently received a letter from a student I'll call Hannah that articulates how students feel about the way adults perceive them.

Dear Mr. Beaudoin,

My name is Hannah and I am a 2003 graduate of Kennebunk High School. This letter is regarding my appreciation for the many positive changes that you have brought to Kennebunk throughout my last two years of high school. It was nice to have an authoritative figure in charge that cared enough about the school and its students to make the changes that you did.

In my first two years of high school the rules and regulations were very restrictive. I know that a school can only be as lenient as the most misbehaving student will let it be. However, most of the other students and I felt that they were never given a chance to prove ourselves responsible to make the rules more lenient.

Thank you for giving us this chance. For example, extending the lunch periods. Not only was it a good time to relax and take a

(cont'd.)

break from the seven-hour day, but you also gave us the freedom to eat where we felt most comfortable. Whether this was your intent or not, by giving high school students that freedom, we got a chance to take responsibility for ourselves and prove that we could handle it.

Also, a great opportunity you created was the New York Exchange Program. It was a learning opportunity for the entire school community to bring people from a different place with different backgrounds into a place, like Kennebunk, with very little diversity. It was even more of an experience for the students from our school who got the chance to experience life in the city. None of this would have been possible without a leader like you, who takes an idea and puts it into action.

I congratulate you for all the great ideas you've had in trying to make KHS a better learning environment and making a more enjoyable place to be. At the end of my senior year I had definitely grown enough to move and make my next step in life. However, I wasn't as enthusiastic about leaving Kennebunk as I thought I would be. In all actuality I was a little disappointed that I was going to miss out on the changes that would be happening in the near future. For the most part this is all thanks to you and the participating faculty that made KHS such a memorable place. Keep up the good work.

Sincerely,

Hannah

I found this letter especially poignant because I had to look up Hannah's yearbook picture to remember who she was. She hadn't stood out as a scholar, an athlete, a school leader, or a student with challenging behaviors. When I showed the letter to her counselor, I learned that Hannah had overcome some major personal obstacles while completing high school. Yet from her college dorm room, she was thoughtful enough to share her reflections about her high school days with me.

Hannah's letter shows how much students value opportunities to prove themselves responsible and trustworthy. Because we want students to be responsible, we must give them occasions to practice responsibility. Because we want them to act respectfully, we must respect and appreciate them. When we believe in their abilities, students deliver. When we trust them, and they know it, we can allocate our resources of time and energy far differently.

It wasn't any earth-shattering innovation that changed Hannah's view of high school. Quite simply, she noticed our efforts to trust her and to believe in what she and her classmates could do. She felt like a possibility—not a problem!

The graph in Figure 3 shows how students viewed the behavior of their classmates as the school gave them more freedom and responsibility.

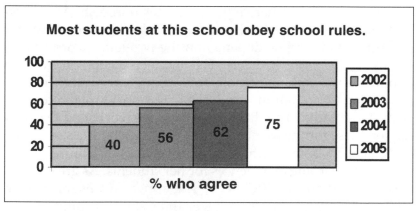

Figure 3

Inspiration versus Control

In my early days as a basketball coach, I discovered that my players performed better when correctly motivated. The more I acted like a drillmaster, the less my players responded. They played with greater determination and passion when I could inspire them, yet when I became too authoritative, their response was lackluster.

My experiences in eight different school systems have yielded ample evidence that educators who insist on control miss out on the opportunity to inspire. Many teachers and administrators seem convinced that order and control are the foundation of a great classroom and great schools. It is hard for them to trust that the opposite can be true—great classrooms and great schools are the foundation for order and control.

In and of itself, control is certainly not a negative thing. It is an absolute necessity as we strive to keep schools safe and orderly. Student voice will not thrive in a school that is out of control. Schools plagued by racial tension, a climate of disrespect, or violence must be made safe before these dreams of student responsibility can be realized. Young people need clear boundaries, and they need experiences with penalties and rewards.

But often, in an effort to make schools secure, administrators end up making them restrictive. As soon as the environment becomes insensitive or harsh, the outcomes diminish. At a classroom management seminar years ago, I heard someone say that high-quality discipline depends on the two-letter word *no* and on saying that word with *love*. This model is a good one to keep in mind as we explore methods to improve school climate.

Anger, intimidation, putdowns, and unsympathetic criticism do not advance educational practice, yet many teachers rely on these for the sake of control or "teaching life's lessons." Long ago, I worked with a truly gifted teacher who provided wonderful learning experiences for her students. As great as she was, she had an Achilles' heel—she appeared unsympathetic and intimidating to students. Over time, she had come to trust that this controlling approach worked for her. What she missed was that her success came from great teaching strategies, solid planning, and inspirational lessons, rather than from her tight control. Her contributions to her students might have been so much greater had she caught on to this idea early in her career.

This teacher misused control within an environment of great teaching. Unfortunately, control is the staple of teachers who are not so good at their craft. This is when students really suffer. Under the weight of a controlling climate, schools fail to thrive. We must find ways to help school leaders—indeed, all who work in our classrooms—realize the difference between inspiration and control. We must find ways to increase the former and let go of the latter. In my experience, the key is to have students truly engaged in their educational program and their school.

Recently my leadership team and I had an opportunity to practice what we preach. At a meeting a few days after the homecoming dance, someone raised the subject of the dancing scene. Five of us on duty at the dance had left questioning the way some of our young people were dancing. I later described it to a student leadership group as extreme MTV club-type dancing—something they would never do if their parents were watching. Their dance moves might have been okay in a nightclub, but not on our administrative watch—not in our high school gymnasium.

The administrative team concluded that we had to do something. If we ignored the dancing we had seen, the issue might well intensify over time. Two apparent solutions were to set standards for dance behavior in the form of new rules or to stage a series of heart-to-heart meetings with the worst offenders—remedies that would have helped us gain control of the situation.

Instead, we turned to our student forum, a group of 68 students who represent our advisory groups. We drafted a letter, humorously entitled "Lords of the Dance," describing how the behavior we had witnessed during the homecoming dance had made us uncomfortable. Noting how much we enjoy chaperoning these events because of the phenomenal student turnout and the fun that our students experience, we pointed out that the last thing we wanted to do was create restrictive rules and spend the evening policing student compliance. We concluded by expressing our belief that the best solution for us involved handing the dilemma over to them.

There was little reaction as the letter was read. The students seemed to totally understand our situation. Some discussion followed, leading us to look at the issue from different perspectives. There was talk about generation gaps, the MTV culture, and parental expectations of school personnel—Elvis Presley even cropped up in the conversation.

The large group reached a consensus that student groups should do something before the school's next big dance, the

Snowball. One senior who was a student council member and also an officer of the class organizing the dance offered to take charge. She agreed to talk to her leadership groups and come back to me with ideas. The suggestions included discussion of dance expectations during advisory meetings, cautionary messages printed on the Snowball tickets, and editorials in the student newspaper.

None of the students balked at these ideas. They clearly seemed pleased that we had not tried to control them by jamming a bunch of rules down their throats. It would be a stretch to suggest that they felt inspired to change the culture of dance in our school—but they certainly understood that they had a choice about, or a responsibility for, toning down their dance behaviors. They also understood that we had responsibilities for setting boundaries and appreciating our attempt to convey those with love.

Prisoners or Volunteers

In our efforts to change schools for the better, we must strive to get students to become volunteers in school structures that often imprison them. We cannot hope to achieve the same level of motivation with inmates that we can with volunteers. Therefore, we must find ways to give our students a spirit of volunteerism.

The notion of making a difference spurs people to action. How can we get students to believe they can make a difference, in a world that sometimes appears indifferent to young people? How can we give them authentic opportunities to contribute to their community? It's not that youngsters lack kindness; rather, they lack the opportunity to act on their compassion. The same can be said for their decision-making or problem-solving abilities—skills that will lie dormant if we doubt their existence.

I'd like to share just a couple of examples of what young people can accomplish. Several advisory groups in our school recently created holiday baskets with cookies and thank-you notes for our custodial and maintenance staff. This was more than a thoughtful gesture—as word of their generosity spread throughout the community, the idea expanded, and the baskets even included a gift certificate for a massage!

In another instance, a student representative to our school board solved a problem that had plagued us for years, namely the need to have our students take state-level standardized testing more seriously. We suspected that some students were not giving these tests their best effort because the scores had no real impact on them individually. We debated whether to include these test results on student transcripts. Some thought this would motivate better effort, while others argued that the scores could hurt students in the college search process. The student board member offered a completely sensible compromise: We should reward students who meet or exceed state standards by including state scores on their transcripts only. This would help those students, inspire all students to strive to meet the standards, and not hurt anyone.

Schools can change the view of students as noncontributors by practicing one simple principle: Define the school as the students' community. Any school's program offers ample opportunities for volunteerism. Students can tutor others, recycle, beautify their building, support one another, and promote compassion for a variety of causes. The notion of service, modeled and practiced within the school, can then expand to a larger community.

We've heard a lot lately about how today's students are immersed in an instant gratification society. As schools struggle to engage them, one strategy is to give them opportunities to feel important. The sense that they are making a difference can compete effectively with the novelty and stimulation of contemporary culture. Success in authentic individual contributions can vie with the thrill of achieving the next level on some electronic game.

With a little forethought, schools can fashion many paths for students to provide service within their school and the wider community. The key is to believe that students can make a difference.

2

Changing the Practice

When I speak at conferences and workshops about the power of student voice, I receive fairly consistent feedback. Participants find the concept inspiring, and many are eager to take steps toward elevating student voice at their schools. But some are leery of the work involved. I distinctly remember one high school principal who only wished he didn't have to deal with teacher evaluations, budget problems, and discipline issues so he could do great things with student voice initiatives. He sees enhancing student voice as just another program. He cannot embark on the journey because his suitcase is already full.

But he missed the point. Student voice is not one more item to cram into his suitcase. It's an attitude, an approach. All he needs to do is fold his clothes differently—repack his suitcase, and set off.

In fact, student voice makes almost everything else in school easier to accomplish. If students are positive about school, engaged in their learning, and invested in school programs, an educational leader's job is noticeably easier. Student voice can impact student discipline; student voice can impact teacher evaluation. These are compelling incentives for changing past practices in favor of a student-centered approach.

Step Outside the Comfort Zone

As school leaders, we are often tempted to strive for a tranquil environment. But, as Dennis Littky wrote, "A silent school is not a school at all."[5] Without question, encouraging student voice contains an element of risk. It takes courage to unconditionally listen to students, to empower them, and to trust that they will do great things.

As we take the first steps toward unleashing student voice, we should anticipate some messiness. Students may be slow to react; they may not trust that adults are really sincere about giving them power. Or they may start campaigning for frivolous changes—an open campus, or soft drink dispensers in each classroom. But with patience, resolve, and some planning, school leaders can minimize the initial mess.

In an address to local students at a National Honor Society induction ceremony, English teacher Thom Ingraham encouraged them to "make sure that the mistakes they made were interesting." He stressed that mistakes were (inevitably) in their future, and the challenge was to make them in areas that would be worthwhile. That advice applies to school leaders who set out to elevate student voice. The journey might be a bit untidy at times, but it is a journey well worth taking.

The Kennebunk High School student newspaper, *Ramblings*, recently featured the concept of student voice in our school. In six articles and editorials, there was not one mention of student voice as a negative or undesirable venture. Instead, the student writers encouraged other students to get involved in school affairs. That's as good as it gets.

The Leader Sets the Tone

As a school embarks on the journey of promoting student voice, the leader sets the tone. Of course, effective leadership comes in a wide variety of styles, but in my experience, the old autocratic, authoritarian, unapproachable model of leadership does not serve schools well. Certainly, the principal has both power and responsibility. But leaders have a choice in how they set up meetings, how they encourage others to speak, how much they decide to listen, and how willing they are to empathize with

---

[5] Dennis Littky, *The Big Picture: Education is Everyone's Business*, 2004.

others. I believe that leaders should listen more than talk, care more than judge, and understand more than guess.

Imagine how students would respond if they were repeatedly told that their principal wants to listen to them! When students begin to trust that we will listen, they come to believe that what they say has value. The climate in the school shifts from authoritarian to democratic.

On the other hand, after inviting students to speak, we cannot turn and pass harsh verdicts on their ideas. In a society bent on keeping score and passing judgment, school leaders must work hard to create a setting that emphasizes caring. I often catch myself asking a student, "Hey, how are you doing?" and then walking right on. To honor student voice, we must practice waiting for the answer.

Finally, leaders must understand more than guess. In many aspects of a principal's job, this simply means making decisions based on knowledge, data, and experience. When it comes to elevating student voice, it has a deeper meaning. Of course, scores and statistics tell us a good deal about our students. But to really know them, we must listen to them. Listen, and value what they say. Listen, and value who they are.

In the worlds of business, sport, and history, models of leadership abound, and we can learn from them. Consider the decisions that Sir Ernest Shackleton made to keep his crew alive during his Antarctic expedition.[6] Thankfully, we don't have to deal with bitter cold, isolation, lack of food, and threats of mutiny—but we do face our share of daily crises and conflicts, and how we respond makes a difference.

Choose Your Attitude

The FISH! Philosophy,[7] a way to look at work and life made famous by Pike's Place Fish Market in Seattle, promotes the idea that you can choose your attitude. You can get up in the morning and choose to be miserable, or you can choose to be upbeat

---

[6] Caroline Alexander, *The Endurance*, 1999.
[7] Charthouse Learning.com.

and happy. Our attitudes toward school and students also come down to a simple choice.

I get up every morning and make a concerted effort to put kids first. It might not always be possible; perhaps a family member is ill, or my car battery is dead. But on most days, I can choose to put kids first. This plays out in everything that I do. I might invite a teacher to reframe a complaint in the context of what is best for our students. I might set aside finalizing a budget proposal to stroll through the hallways at dismissal time. The number one rule for booking my appointments is that I drop everything if a student wants to see me. No, I wouldn't reschedule a meeting with the school board chair or superintendent, but students come first in my book.

Likewise, creating a school climate that embraces student voice begins with a choice. You have to decide that it is important and then set about to change what you do. James O. Prochaska[8] identifies the stages of change as precontemplation, contemplation, preparation, action, maintenance, and termination. These stages occur in a spiral rather than a straight line; you can cycle through them more than once as you work to change behavior. You might have to start over, maybe again and again. Also, because each member of your organization moves at a different pace through this continuum, you may have to keep reminding yourself and them of the choices that set you on this path.

For of course, you can't achieve substantial change on your own, or in a vacuum. Choosing your attitude is a great concept, but you must also understand the beliefs and attitudes of others—and give them persuasive reasons to do the work. In my experience, the most compelling argument for promoting student voice is the possibility of increasing student engagement. What teacher would not want students to be motivated? What parent would object to children feeling invested in their education?

Theodore Sizer, founder of the Coalition of Essential Schools, talks of educators "marshalling students to the cause."

---

[8] James O. Prochaska et al., *Changing for Good*, 1994.

In my experience, students rally to the cause of education that works for them, schools that put students first, and adults who welcome student voice.

No Secrecy, No Surprises

We want students involved in their education, invested in their school. It only makes sense, then, to keep them informed about school improvement plans. Unfortunately, many students are surprised as one change after another is sprung upon them. Consider the following scenarios.

All schools strive to create a safe and orderly environment for their students and staff. Many schools, particularly since the Columbine tragedy, have installed some sort of security cameras. Many a school has done so without advance notice, only to be met by a storm of objections when students discover the devices. How do you get students to see such measures not as an intrusion, a violation of their rights, but as a way to protect them and deter vandalism? You do this by including them in the discussion ahead of time.

In my experience, talking things out in advance makes an important difference to school climate. When we decided to purchase a Breathalyzer to deter students from coming to dances under the influence, we discussed the idea openly. When we moved to reduce passing time between classes, we first pointed out that this would allow students to have an earlier dismissal. Both ideas received student support because we worked in a climate of openness.

Obviously, some decisions and changes cannot involve a great deal of negotiation with students. People who are leery of student voice and democratic practices in schools fear that students would end up running the school. In my experience, students still look to adults for guidance, for establishing boundaries, and for discipline, even in the most democratic of settings. They understand that not all decisions can be left to them. The key to keeping students on your side lies not in giving them what they want, but in standing ready to discuss matters that are important to them. School leaders who involve students in the discussion, explain changes thoroughly, and avoid springing things on students generally get their support. Students come to believe that decisions are made in their best interest and, as often as possible, with their input.

The Earlier, the Better

Over the years, I have reaped the rewards of promoting student voice. Students have cooperated with me as a teacher and a principal in school after school, grateful that I have listened to their voices. But I should not have stood out. High school students should not feel honored when the principal or the faculty allows them to have a voice. By the time they get to high school, students should be veterans of the democratic process. It should be a foregone conclusion that it is their school, that they have a stake in decision-making, and that they contribute to the larger community. The earlier our students discover their voices, the better.

Even the youngest of students can learn the skills of leadership, citizenship, and participatory democracy. We need not wait for some magical age. Elementary and middle schools that promote citizenship pave the way for even better programming around student involvement in high schools. At any level, morning meetings, student round tables, responsive classrooms, and other such practices provide students with opportunities to practice civic engagement.

Years ago, our son was struggling with fifth grade. My wife and I scheduled an appointment with his teacher, hoping to gain some insight about bringing more joy to his days. We had planned to start the meeting without our son, then call him in later. But he had a different idea. He attended the entire meeting; in fact, he ran it. The outcome was outstanding. Our son was able to articulate what was bothering him about school, and his teacher was able to support some changes that would eventually make a difference for him. Given the opportunity, even a fifth grader can advocate for himself.

I was quite impressed with Stephen Covey's latest book, *The 8th Habit*. I found his ideas congenial (his eighth habit has to do with finding our voice and inspiring others to find theirs). What is more, the accompanying DVD presented sixteen inspirational companion films, one of which provides an excellent example of student voice. One of the film clips, *AB Combs*[9], effectively shows young children at AB Combs Elementary School in Raleigh, North Carolina, speaking at an assembly honoring Dr. Covey. Youngsters from first grade up approached the microphone and gave short personal accounts of how Covey's writings applied to them. It seemed fitting that children took center stage, and their inclusion clearly illustrates the confidence we should have in the ability of our youth.

It's Not about the Recipe

People often ask whether promoting student voice would work in alternative settings. Most of my experiences in administration have occurred at small high schools in rural or suburban settings in the Northeast. It's natural to ask how these ideas would transfer to larger urban schools. I have spent some time in urban schools and can appreciate how some of their challenges differ from those I have known. Cupcakes are not wedding cakes—but they have much in common.

For several years, I have been involved with an exchange program with high schools in the New York City borough of Brooklyn. During this exchange, students from Maine are exposed to an entirely different world. From a high school of 850, relatively large by Maine standards, they spend time in city schools with over 3,000 students. Most of the Maine students are white; in the city schools they visit, almost 80 percent are students of color. The New York City students find novelty in quiet streets and the darkness of starlit nights. They spend some time in homes that have all the conveniences of their neighborhoods under one roof. One Brooklyn student, Shawn, marveled at the fact that his host family lived in a home with a well stocked refrigerator, a pool table, and Nintendo games. In the city, he would ordinarily leave his apartment for meals, recreation, and

---

[9] Franklin Covey Co., 2004.

entertainment. But both groups recognize that these differences in customs and cultures are superficial. Whatever the setting, students have the same fundamental needs.

I'm reminded of Lance Armstrong's bestseller, *It's Not About the Bike*.[10] Cycling enthusiasts, hoping to gain from Armstrong's biking and training secrets, rushed out to buy his book. But Armstrong wrote about cycling in the framework of much broader topics—overcoming cancer, relationships, celebrity. He couldn't have laid out the one sure formula for winning the Tour de France. Likewise, there's no one recipe for promoting student voice. It's not a matter of measuring out exactly the same ingredients in exactly the same order. The chef must understand the environment and the issues and make decisions accordingly. But certain ingredients belong in the recipe, whatever the setting.

One fundamental ingredient is safety. Student voice does not mean that students are left to their own devices to falter and face disappointment. Their voices must be protected and cultivated. Schools must offer guided situations that allow for mistakes in low-stakes conditions. Adults must create an environment that keeps students safe from ridicule, fraud, and dismissal.

In an attempt to increase student involvement and leadership, one high school invited students to develop a new dress code policy for school board approval. After months of work, the student council presented its plan to the school board, only to have it voted down. Student voice in this school suffered a debilitating blow because the board was not ready for student proposals. This is not to say that school boards must approve any student-proposed plan, but they ought to at least embrace the notion that students can impact policy—and schools setting out to promote student voice would be well advised to begin with an issue less controversial than the dress code.

Even where student voice finds an audience, adults must take care not to ask too much of students. Students can play a role in increasing respect for diversity or reducing low-level bullying, but longstanding racial issues or gang warfare present

---

[10] Lance Armstrong, *It's Not About the Bike*, 2002.

thornier challenges. Adults have the responsibility to keep students safe. As one student put it, "Adults should be like bumpers on a bowling lane, ensuring that the ball does not go into the gutter."

Commit to the Journey

I am willing to step outside my comfort zone and seek to lead by listening, caring and understanding.

I will choose to see students as possibilities rather than problems.

I will seek to inspire more than to control.

Consequently, my students will see themselves as volunteers rather than prisoners-young people with the skills and knowledge needed to sustain our democracy.

In a climate highlighted by trust, we will work to further our mission of creating

- ◆ *a school for each kid*
- ◆ *a school that promotes a sense of belonging and accomplishment*
- ◆ *a school that gets students to care.*

3

Paying Heed to Student Voice

It's All about Choices

Parenting taught me a great deal about how children tick. If you ask a toddler whether she wants to brush her teeth before or after she puts on her pajamas, she will probably brush her teeth without much fuss. The seven-year old can complete his chores with more gusto if he knows that he will read a book or kick a soccer ball around with dad when he's through. Choices and alternatives increase motivation and promote empowerment. Youngsters love the feeling that they have choices about things that impact them. This desire for autonomy does not subside as kids walk through the schoolhouse gate.

✴ We want students to act responsibly. Therefore, we must give them choices—opportunities to make decisions that lead to commitment and ownership. Within each lesson plan, within each classroom, within each school, educators can give students a chance to practice responsibility, independence, and autonomy.

The strongest connection between the lessons we learn as parents and the challenges we face as educators lies in the words so often heard when small children burst into tears, or grab a toy from a friend, or kick or hit or throw something: "Use your words." What a breakthrough moment arrives when the toddler starts to express concerns clearly! "I have a boo-boo."

"He grabbed my truck." "I want to swing." "I want more juice." And, with greater sophistication, "I want to do it by myself." "I'm scared of the spider." "It's not fair." "I miss Daddy." The communication skills our children learn in the kitchen and on the playground can carry them far in school—if we honor their voices in that arena.

In *Sometimes a Shining Moment: The Foxfire Experience*,[11] Eliot Wigginton offers a number of instructional practices to enhance teaching. I'm struck by how many of these practices also enhance student voice. Here are ten core practices:

1. All teacher and student work flows from student desire and student concerns.

2. The teacher is not the boss, but a collaborator, group leader, and guide.

3. The academic integrity of the work must be clear.

4. Students are not merely receivers of processed information; their work is active.

5. The focus is on teamwork, group work and peer teaching.

6. Work connects to the student's community and the real world.

7. Student work must have an audience beyond the teacher.

8. New activities spiral from previous ones rather than occurring as disjointed projects.

9. Students must be given aesthetic experiences, where imagination and sense of accomplishment lead to rich outcomes.

10. All work includes time and processes that promote student reflection.

---

[11] Eliot Wigginton, *Sometimes a Shining Moment: The Foxfire Experience*, 1986.

Clearly, teachers play a critical role in promoting student voice. They set the tone in the classroom; they write the lesson plans; they frame the discussions; they assess the outcomes. They can give students choices along the way—choices in the development of classroom rules, choices among various methods of assessment, and so forth. A school can build a culture of honoring student voice only if teachers buy into the endeavor at the grassroots level.

In this chapter, we'll focus on the many opportunities for teachers and school leaders to heed student voices within the formal structure of the school day. Surveys and advisories, town meetings and the principal's open-door policy, student-led parent conferences and student feedback to teachers all offer valuable channels for students to "use their words" as they take responsibility for their own education.

The Survey Says . . .

A highlight of graduation week at Kennebunk High School is the premiere of the senior video—usually a 30-minute production that showcases student actors, student screenwriting, and student filmmaking skills. In the 2004 film, a corrupt power plotted to overtake the school. Faced with a perplexing problem, the student playing the role of principal rubbed his chin and proclaimed, "I think I'll conduct a survey on this matter." The audience broke out in laughter, hoots, and cheers. It was a huge inside joke: At KHS, school leaders relied on surveys of student opinion as a standard approach to problem solving. Some students complained that we surveyed them to death, but most appreciated the way we valued student voice.

Surveys—election polls, straw ballots, opinion polls, and the like—are common in many venues, including schools. But they can backfire. If school leaders aren't prepared to act on the results, they probably shouldn't take a survey. (Don't ask students what time school should start unless you have the authority to change the bus schedule.) Unless students trust that their voices matter, they'll simply dismiss surveys as a waste of time.

Another critical component of effective surveying is to publish the results promptly. This demonstrates that you value the responses, but it has another effect that is subtler and more powerful: It shows people how their outlook lines up with the outlook of others. Often, dissension simmers because people simply do not have an accurate picture of what others really believe. A survey that brings clarity to majority and minority views can pave the way for acceptance of administrative action—or even acceptance of different ways of thinking.

Finally, repeating the same survey can help to identify changes in attitudes and outcomes over time—a powerful leverage point in validating success or creating compelling reasons for change. Several years ago, when trying to establish a stronger advisory program, leaders at our school conducted a ten-question survey of student attitudes about steps we had taken. In the initial survey, student opinions were evenly distributed across the spectrum from negative to positive. When we asked the same ten questions a year later, the responses were overwhelmingly positive. The changes had clearly won acceptance, fueling our commitment to further improvement.

Of course, surveys have their limits. The questions may contain a bias; the results may be reported in misleading ways. Even well-designed surveys may not yield statistically significant results or startling insights. Some may simply record the obvious, wasting everyone's time. Most educators who connect well with kids can accurately predict what students think and want. But when students see that you care enough to ask, and when they believe that what they say matters, surveys are worth their weight in gold.

Advisory: Students Speak, We Listen

I have been involved in creating, revamping, and restoring advisory programs in five different schools. Developing an effective advisory program is among the hardest journeys a school can embark on, and I've made my share of mistakes. But I have found that bringing students together with adults who know them as individuals can play a powerful role in elevating student voice.

The groups need not be formal. The early-morning gathering of students in Mr. J's room certainly qualified, in many ways, as a climate conducive to student voice. Call it what you like—homeroom, home base, or advisory—and set whatever program expectations meet your students' needs. I have found that such student groupings effectively cultivate student voice as long as they meet four criteria: size, frequency, duration, and permission.

"Small is beautiful" when it comes to education. Large schools strive to create smaller communities of learning, and districts work to pass budgets that minimize class sizes. Likewise, student-teacher ratio is an important consideration when developing advisory groups. In my experience, the magic number is twelve students to one adult, though a group might occasionally creep to thirteen or fourteen. In most schools, attaining numbers this low may mean calling on nonteaching personnel to serve as advisors or adult leaders. A custodian or a secretary, an administrator or a cook, a counselor or an educational technician can be an effective adult mentor. Keeping groups small is an essential first step in establishing a climate where kids are willing and able to have a voice.

The next consideration is frequency—how often student groups come together. The formula is simple: The more frequently, the better. A daily meeting is a wonderful regularity; strive for at least three times a week. The old homeroom model of weekly or biweekly sessions simply does not offer enough listening time—time for personal conversations to crop up, time for student voice to prosper.

The principle of duration is even more straightforward. The typical seven- or eight-minute homeroom period will not do. Taking attendance and listening to daily announcements crowd out any personal communication. Advisory programs or other organizational setups that provide time for impromptu discussion usually allow fifteen minutes or more. I've had experience with daily advisory periods eighteen or nineteen minutes long—plenty of time to encourage student voice.

Finally, there is the matter of permission. For student voice to have a chance, students must be clear about the fact that they can say what they think and feel. This requires more than a formal declaration. Students must trust that adults will really listen—and adults must deliver the goods to establish that climate of trust. At the same time, students must understand that their freedom to speak out comes with the responsibility to speak appropriately.

If students meet with a caring adult often, in small groups, for long enough to talk about things that matter to them, student voice can find expression. In the best scenario, what students say will make a difference in their schools.

An Open Door

In *Stepping Outside Your Comfort Zone: Lessons for School Leaders*, I describe such an incident. Students in one advisory group were worked up because they couldn't use a microwave oven in the cafeteria. Their advisor relayed this concern to the administration, which promptly purchased two microwave ovens and set up a student microwave station in the cafeteria. Word soon spread among students that their voices had been heard. This seemingly unremarkable event must have advanced the notion that students had permission to speak their minds, for shortly thereafter, a bumper crop of students made appointments to talk to me about individual concerns or ideas to improve the school.

I had always welcomed meeting with students, but the microwave incident seemed to have stimulated an urge to communicate. In fact, individual advisors, counselors, and other administrators also reported that students seemed more willing to share what was on their minds. One particular encounter illustrates just how student voice was emerging.

When a senior I'll call Jake made an appointment to see me, I was a bit surprised at first. Jake was not really involved in school activities, and I hadn't had any interaction with him. His advisor, who had listened to his complaints for several weeks, finally convinced him that I was interested in hearing what students thought. Jake entered my office with a long list of gripes. Although he was respectful, I was taken aback at how angry he was. He seemed incensed at every single thing the school did. The complaint I remember most vividly was that school policy required students to ask permission to leave class to go to the bathroom. In a threatening tone, Jake maintained that the school would ultimately be held responsible if he developed problems with bodily functions in his old age.

As I listened to this grievance and a dozen or so others, I tried to explain why we did what we did. I also tried to suggest ways he might look at these matters differently or adjust his behavior so they wouldn't bother him so much. I'm not sure how much it helped. But because I let him vent, because I listened without judging, at least Jake had to cross off his list the major gripe that adults at school didn't listen to him.

Let's Talk about It Together

As part of our plans for advisory each year, we included six or seven school-wide discussion activities. On a set date, all advisories would formally discuss the same subject matter. Typical topics might be school vandalism and the consideration of security cameras, or the school's policy on academic honesty. To support advisors who were apprehensive about facilitating group discussions, we gave them a graphic organizer that they could use as a guide to generate student comments. The outcomes in these activities were as varied as the number of groups, but there was a universal consistency: Every student knew that we valued what they thought—because we took the time to ask.

These school-wide discussions yielded some nice results. When we talked about bullying in school or the impact of cliques on school climate, the dialogue alone created some subtle changes. When the conversation addressed creating a better atmosphere in the school cafeteria, we didn't see immediate improvement, but at least the situation in the cafeteria didn't get worse. In many advisory groups, students started talking about school issues spontaneously. Students began to take a more active role in school affairs. They started taking our invitations to get involved more seriously.

In a recent Oprah Winfrey interview, Barbara Walters commented that "quality time" with her daughter meant more than

being there on all the important occasions. The richness of relationships lies in the unstructured time, the spontaneous time—
riding in a car, or sitting on a beach. This is so true of my
experiences with advisory programs. Many of the best outcomes occur when students are not forced to discuss things.
Once students are in a comfortable setting, they fill up the silence and the down time with their valuable voices.

Advisors and the School Also Benefit

One goal of an advisory program is simply to ensure that no
student goes through school unnoticed. Good advisors go
beyond that, but this need not be a complicated matter. I liken it
to the role of a coach: Much as a coach helps an athletic team
pursue a championship season, the advisor helps students set
and pursue academic and personal goals.

Advisory programs, set up to support students, end up ben-
efiting advisors and the school as well. As students talk about
their social and academic experiences, advisors gain a wider
view of our school. As advisors listen with care, they become
more than subject-area teachers and classroom managers—they
become teachers of people, advocates for their advisees.

Consider what happens when a student shares a concern
with an advisor and the advisor helps the student address that
concern. The assistance might be as simple as meeting with another teacher to mediate a situation—perhaps speaking with a
science teacher about a student's problem with test anxiety. But
each time advisors help individual students in this way, they
also encourage student voice, student self-advocacy.

Student-Led Conferences

One of the best ways to promote student voice is to have
students plan the conversations between the school and their
parents at conference time. This represents a huge departure
from traditional practice, which usually involves the parents
and the teacher talking about the absent student. Student-led
conferences put students front and center. In my experience,

showcasing students in this way boosts parent turnout to more than 80 percent.

Student-led conferences also provide students with excellent practice for performance exhibitions and college and job interviews. A college admissions officer once commented that many high school graduates struggle to articulate who they are. When asked to talk formally about their skills, goals, or learning, even strong students can be reduced to two- and three-word sentences. Students need to be trained to advocate for themselves, and student-led conferences provide that training.

The letter shown here illustrates one way to introduce this protocol to parents.

November 5, 2002

Dear Parent/Guardian:

We are sending this letter to provide more information about student-led conferences (SLCs), which will take place at KHS on November 26 and 27. We will first review why we feel this new program is so important. Second, we will try to alleviate some concerns parents may have about this new procedure. Last, we will offer suggestions on how you can help us achieve success. The reasons behind instituting student-led conferences fall in three broad categories: They increase parental participation; they put your students in the center of the process; and they help our young people make stronger connections between school and personal goals.

It has been said that high-achieving schools have high levels of parental involvement, and we are hoping for 100% support from our parents in this endeavor. We also know that student ownership in the educational process is critical to academic success. We want our students to be able to articulate who they are, where they are going, and what they need to do to get there.

As we strive to improve the quality of teaching at Kennebunk High School through reflective practice, we also want to stress the need for our students to be reflective about their learning.

(cont'd.)

We recognize that some parents have concerns about this change. Although we would like you to go along with us despite your apprehension, some clarification is in order. The following represent some common concerns and our efforts to put parents at ease:

1. I ALREADY HAVE RICH EDUCATIONAL DISCUSSIONS WITH MY STUDENT. I DO NOT SEE THE NEED TO PARTICIPATE.

   We understand that some of our families have high-level educational conversations in their homes, and we applaud that. The formality of SLCs, however, should provide your student with valuable training for college and job interviews, make them the initiators of the conversation, and provide parents with more insight into their personal plans. The bottom line here is that many of our families do not have rich conversations about school, and they need to if we are going to improve our school.

2. I LIKED THE OLD METHOD OF MEETING WITH MY CHILD'S TEACHERS, AND I DON'T THINK THIS STUDENT-LED IDEA WILL MEET MY NEEDS.

   Please understand that teachers will communicate with you via phone, email, or conference at your request. We are not saying that we won't do this. What we are saying is that you may not feel such a conference is necessary following our student-led conferences. You will find that your student is capable of articulating what is happening in terms of his/her class work and will even be able to make commitments to needed changes. Please give this a chance to work, with the understanding that you can always contact individual teachers afterwards with questions and concerns. (Our last experience with this ended with only five requests to meet with individual teachers, after over 700 conferences!)

3. MY STUDENT APPEARS TO BE REALLY STRUGGLING WITH SCHOOL. I AM NOT SURE THAT WE WILL GET ANY RESULTS FROM THIS CONFERENCE.

   We hope that all of our students will be able to accentuate some positives during their conferences. We know that some students are struggling, and we also know that our old conference structure did not have a major impact on this. We believe that success comes from identifying issues, developing action plans, and giving our students new hope. Student-led conferences may indeed help our struggling students a great deal. Parental support through conference attendance would be an excellent first step.

We would like to offer some suggestions on how all parents can help this program succeed.

1.) Some of our students will be less than forthcoming with information about conferences.

   Ask them for information.

2.) Some of our students will come to school insisting that their parents won't do this.

   Tell them that you have every intention of doing this.

3.) Some of our students will be quite nervous about participating.

   Try to put them at ease. Point out that this will not be a judgmental process.

4.) This is new to everyone (staff, students, and parents) and is occurring in a short timeline.

   We all need to be forgiving of this first attempt.

5.) If you are going to be out of town on November 26 and 27, *please call your student's advisory teacher to set up another time to do this conference.*

You can expect your student to bring home a conference time sign-up sheet on Tuesday, November 12. Please fill it out and return it on November 13 via your student. If we cannot arrive at a confirmed time through this process, expect a phone call by Sunday, November 17, from your student's advisor.

Thanks for reading this lengthy letter, and thank you in advance for supporting this important program.

Sincerely,

Nelson Beaudoin

Parents had this to say about our student-led conferences:

♦ I think student-led conferences are a dramatic improvement over the traditional conference method. This new system allows for much more specificity and draws the student into the conversation with effective results. Good job to all who had a hand in this very positive change.

♦ This is a valuable process for students. Keep it up!

♦ Excellent conference and opportunity for students to take responsibility for their academic behavior.

♦ For the second year I was very impressed by the preparation and the format of my son's student-led conference. The collection of work, grades and concerns addressed were very appropriate. The advisors were very professional and considerate.

♦ A very positive experience! Our son did a great job; he identified his weaknesses and seemed to take ownership of his education.

♦ I really like the format—kids more involved.

♦ I was very pleased with our student-led conference. My son was willing to contribute in an effective way to his future. That is something I have not seen from him before.

Student Feedback to Teachers

Of all the avenues for student voice in schools, none compares in impact to the feedback students give teachers about instruction. Commendably, many teachers solicit this information daily. But far more teachers hesitate, fearing that students will be self-serving, or less than truthful, or hurtful, or worse. Too often, those who would derive the greatest benefit are least likely to seek student feedback.

Reflection is a vital part of excellence; for teachers, that reflection should include a student perspective. By listening intently to students, teachers can learn more about motivation, the appropriateness of assignments, clues to maximize learning, and the effectiveness of various teaching strategies. Even with these rich rewards, some teachers still can't bring themselves to ask students. Some may feel threatened by the possibility of bad news; others may firmly believe that they know their craft. Some may demand that students sign their evaluation, mistakenly believing that otherwise kids wouldn't be honest. The conflict between inspiration and control exists here as well!

For the past few years, I have encouraged every teacher to enter this feedback loop with students. The process I follow is fairly simple and remarkably nonthreatening: I simply ask teachers to have students fill out the survey tool shown here, or another instrument of their choosing. They are to tally the results and use them privately. I don't expect them to share the results with anyone else (especially me). I just ask them to turn in a form indicating that they have completed the process and noting whether the feedback was helpful. Nearly all comply, and nearly all find the process helpful. Occasionally, one teacher or another shares the feedback with me—either to brag a bit or to get help with issues raised.

In turn, I invite the teaching staff to evaluate my work. My secretary compiles their feedback, and I share the results with them. Although I do not ask that teachers share their results with students, I hope that my actions encourage them to do so. I see great value in letting students see what their classmates are thinking, and sharing the feedback demonstrates that the teacher carefully considers student viewpoints.

Sample Course Feedback Form

The purpose of this form is to gather input from students in order to help teachers improve their teaching. By answering the questions sincerely, you are helping us to improve the instruction at Kennebunk High School. Thank you for your cooperation.

Date _____ Course Title _____ Teacher _____

Your Name (Optional) _____

Please circle the appropriate "grade" for each question.

A= always   B= most of the time   C = sometimes

D= not very often   F= never   N/A= does not apply

1. I understand what is expected.	A	B	C	D	F	N/A
2. The teacher provides a syllabus that is useful.	A	B	C	D	F	N/A
3. The teacher is receptive to answering questions.	A	B	C	D	F	N/A
4. The teacher is enthusiastic about the subject.	A	B	C	D	F	N/A
5. Class work and assignments relate to real life whenever possible.	A	B	C	D	F	N/A
6. Tests and quizzes are fair.	A	B	C	D	F	N/A
7. Assignments are challenging.	A	B	C	D	F	N/A
8. The teacher has a positive attitude toward students.	A	B	C	D	F	N/A
9. Activities are related to subject matter.	A	B	C	D	F	N/A
10. The teacher is available for extra help.	A	B	C	D	F	N/A
11. Grading is fair	A	B	C	D	F	N/A
12. Assignments are returned in a timely fashion.	A	B	C	D	F	N/A
13. The teacher provides clear directions.	A	B	C	D	F	N/A
14. The teacher goes over results of quizzes, tests, written assignments, etc.						
15. The teacher expects me to stay on task throughout the class.	A	B	C	D	F	N/A

16. Class activities require me to think, problem solve, and work hard.	A	B	C	D	F	N/A
17. The teacher avoids intentional personal putdowns against students.	A	B	C	D	F	N/A
18. The teacher uses a variety of resources beyond the textbook, such as group work, projects, multimedia.	A	B	C	D	F	N/A
19. I am prepared for class.	A	B	C	D	F	N/A
20. I work hard in class.	A	B	C	D	F	N/A
21. I know what is expected for me to do well in this class.	A	B	C	D	F	N/A
22. I go in for extra help when I need it.	A	B	C	D	F	N/A

The pace used to cover the material is . . .

circle one   too slow   too fast   just right

Which activities/assignments are <u>most helpful</u> to your learning in this class?

Which activities/assignments are <u>least helpful</u> to your learning in this class?

What do you <u>enjoy most</u> about this class?

What do you <u>enjoy least</u> about this class?

Would you take another course from this teacher? Why or why not?

What changes, if any, would you recommend for this class?

Would you recommend this class to a friend? Why or why not?

Student Speakers

The last of the formal opportunities for students to "use their words" comes when we give them the stage at public events like graduation. Early on in my career, I worried about giving students a microphone and a captive audience. I had visions of students venturing off into inappropriate areas, making outlandish statements, embarrassing the school. I no longer get stressed in these situations, because I no longer try to control them. Here's why.

On one occasion a graduation speaker did cross the line. The student—I'll call him Brad—was entitled to speak based on the standing practice that the top four students had speaking parts. Ranked fourth in his class, Brad was headed to an Ivy League college. Though extremely bright, he was not much of a conformist. He had not established a great reputation with faculty, and he appeared to have a chip on his shoulder when it came to school rules and procedures. As an assistant principal, I was in charge of graduation practice. Based on what I knew about Brad, my concern about student speakers was at an all-time high.

Ordinarily, the senior speakers worked on their speeches with a member of our English faculty during the week of graduation rehearsals, staying after marching practice to run through their speeches. Any controversial or questionable material would surface, and the faculty mentor would help the students refine their work. As graduation approached, I would receive a hard copy of the speech and could relax a bit—though I made it a point to remind the speakers to make their families proud as they stood center stage.

I never received a copy of Brad's speech. Each time I inquired about it, Brad just reassured me that his speech would be excellent—that he would never think of embarrassing himself in front of a thousand people. On the night of graduation, I went up to the speakers, as I always did, and wished them well (no doubt with a final warning as the hidden message). Shaking my hand, Brad told me not to worry, his speech was going to be fine.

Brad was the third speaker to approach the podium. He took the microphone out of its stand, grabbed a chair from offstage, plopped himself down, and proceeded to test the microphone by making a noise as if he were passing gas. It only got worse from there. I don't recall exactly what he said, but I do know that he lambasted school administrators for imposing unbearable rules and restrictions and not listening to kids. I know this because later, when I told people how tempted I was to leap from my seat and yank him off stage, they responded that it would only have reinforced his message.

The speech finally ended. Brad went back to his place on the graduation risers to guarded applause, while I sat in the audience, shocked and embarrassed.

What happened next was magnificent. The next speaker strode to the podium, paused and looked back at his classmates on stage behind him, and then peered out into the audience. After a moment of silence, he remarked, "Well, I guess Brad and I did not attend the same high school!" The senior class responded with a standing ovation of support—and I went from anguish to exhilaration in a matter of seconds.

With the experience of many more graduations under my belt, and memories of fifty or so superb student speeches, I no longer find graduation speeches anywhere near as threatening as I once did. Looking back on that day, I recognize that Brad may have had some good points in his speech about how our school was administered, given his perspective. Yes, he abused the forum he was given, but he also unwittingly created an opportunity for many in the audience to celebrate the school's success.

To this day, I still have a faculty member assist students in preparing their speeches, I still get a hard copy in advance, and I still see the speakers right before and remind them about making everyone proud. But I do all this for very different reasons than in my early years. Back then, I was scared to death that students would do it wrong. Now, I am just trying to inspire them to greatness.

Every school administrator has a dreadful story or two to tell about student speakers. Far outweighing these, however, are the many great stories about students in speaking situations. I recall a young man who upstaged a senator and a governor with an inspiring speech on service learning at our state capitol. I remember a graduating senior whose description of her school experience included insightful praise for individual teachers and administrators. One senior who had earned the right to speak got the jitters and wanted to back out, but with his parents' encouragement, he went on to give one of the best graduation addresses I've ever heard. These stories, and many more like them, speak to the wonder of student voice. Given a microphone, an audience, and something to say, students come through. They may not always deliver great speeches, but they always gain an opportunity to grow.

4

Linking Classroom and Community

Rich opportunities for learning unfold when we link the classroom to the wider community, with student voice as the driving force. In this chapter, we'll consider what happens when we invite students to take their place as leaders in their classrooms, learners in their communities, and people who make a difference in their world.

Community Service

Nearly all the schools I have been involved with have had some type of community service program. The programs varied from highly structured credit-based experiences to more loosely organized volunteer programs. Regardless of the configuration, the outcomes for students were generally the same. After serving others, students are inspired and crave additional opportunities to make a difference.

Around the time of national Make a Difference Day in October, one of the schools I worked at had ninth-grade advisory groups perform service projects in the community, rather than attend classes. Since this involved about 200 ninth graders in groups of fifteen scattered across our huge geographical district, the program presented many challenges. Every year we did this, I had second thoughts about putting in the effort needed. Yet each year at the end of the day, I left committed to supporting it for another year. The outcomes were always good. The few organizational glitches or predictable problems were far outweighed by the positive effect the program had on our students.

The October Make a Difference Day set a tone of service for our student body. They were making a difference, they were proving their worth in their neighborhoods, and they were making valuable connections in the community. Stories abound regarding students who ended up finding part-time employment through their involvement, or even solidifying career choices based on their service experience. Most importantly, it establishes an expectation or norm among the students that service is a good thing to do.

At Kennebunk High School, we have a 30-hour community service requirement tied to graduation. Although I personally disagree with required service (because it ceases to be a voluntary contribution), I have seen numerous students do an absolutely fabulous job of aiding in the community. Moreover, the students at KHS do wonderful group service projects revolving around our spirit week activities, or the We Care projects that our advisory groups take on in December. The lengthy list of benefactors from our students' kindness includes not only national causes, such as supporting our troops or sending aid to tsunami-torn nations, but local efforts such as subsidizing proms in two high schools whose communities have had major unemployment issues.

Each and every cause supported by these examples of student service also promotes student voice. Student voice plays into service projects not only during the planning phase, but during the implementation phase as well. Students gain confidence in their abilities through their service contributions, and success typically leads to future opportunities. My experiences in schools, and with my own children, have taught me that students talk loudest when they are thrilled with what they have accomplished. On multiple occasions, I have witnessed incredible increases in student voice while our students have been busy serving others.

Service Learning

Some people think of service learning in terms of a special program added to a school's curriculum—something outside of the normal pedagogy found in our educational institutions. Nothing could be farther from the truth. Service learning is simply a strategy of teaching—a strategy that is much more common than we realize, and one that consistently leads to high levels of student engagement.

I stumbled onto service learning in 1997 when I asked a teacher who had an extra preparation period to explore beginning a community service program at our high school. Within a year's time, this teacher had not just developed a sound community service program—she had laid the foundation for service learning in our school. Three years later, our school was recognized as a National Service Learning Leader School. Teachers who applied this teaching strategy raved about the level of student motivation and positive learning outcomes that ensued.

Service learning is defined as "a method of teaching/learning that challenges students to identify, research, propose, and implement solutions to real needs in their school or community as part of math, science, social studies, etc."[12] It differs from community service in that it includes a component of student planning (student voice) and is closely connected to curriculum and learning standards—elements not readily apparent in community service. The service learning projects in the last two schools where I have worked have followed the KIDS (Kids Involved Doing Service) Consortium model, which stresses three components: student ownership (the students are involved in the planning), academic integrity (the project aligns with academic standards), and apprentice citizenship (the student work addresses a real community need).

The presence of all three components leads to wonderful student outcomes in a broad range of areas. The "student as planner" component is particularly germane to the concept of

---

[12] KIDS Consortium, 2001 (215 Lisbon Street, Lewiston, Maine 04240 and www.kidsconsortium.org).

student voice. Within these projects, students are very much involved in decision-making. Unlike typical teacher-directed instruction, service learning is very much student-centered. Service learning work can be intergenerational, humanitarian, environmental, or civic. The following examples of projects I have seen in recent years illustrate the simplicity and adaptability of this superb teaching strategy.

The Greatest Generation Project

Junior English students spend time researching the World War II generation, meeting with an elderly person, interviewing that person, and eventually trying to tell the person's story in writing. The unit concludes with a breakfast celebration at a local nursing home, where young and old honor the feats of the greatest generation. Guest speakers, student readers, and student performers celebrate a morning of friendship, song, and remembrance. I have been asked each year to say a few words at this culminating event, only to find myself tongue-tied by the amazing scene of people 65 years apart, interacting so completely.

Family Treasures

In the mid-1990s, as home economics was disappearing from the high school curriculum, an inventive teacher developed a very popular course called Fiber and Fabric that partially met the state standards in art instruction. When service learning started to take hold in our school, she developed a semester course called Family Treasures in which students investigated their roots and family trees. They used quilting, photography, and sewing skills to design quilts that were presented to grandparents or other relatives at a performance exhibition marking the course's conclusion. The voice of students was very much accented in this unit, as they were essentially telling their own personal family stories. Students also made winter hats and mittens that they donated to needy youngsters in the community.

Teaching Foreign Language

It has been said that learning is best achieved when students are doing the teaching. In our teaching foreign language program, eleven of our fourth-year language students each adopt a fifth-grade classroom and provide that class with approximately 20 hours of foreign language instruction during the spring semester. Students are responsible for planning lessons for students who would otherwise have no exposure to a foreign language. The course was started as our school committee struggled with finding a way to move language instruction down to a lower grade level without additional funding. The program benefited the older students, the younger students, and the entire community, with no financial burden to the district.

Wetland Mitigation

In the mid-1990s, we were building a new high school that required wetland mitigation. To compensate for disruption to an existing wetland on site, we had to develop a wetland elsewhere. Rather than pay an exorbitant price to have this done professionally, we wrote a plan that involved our environmental science class overseeing the developing wetland—classifying vegetation, planting special species, and tracking progress over time. The students learned many science skills, worked in meaningful ways to support their new school, and saved the district a substantial amount of money.

Jump Rope for Heart

Each year my wife Sharon, an elementary physical education teacher, coordinates a jumprope marathon involving first, second, and third graders to benefit the American Heart Association. This is a great community service project, but so much more. Sharon deals with aerobic fitness and healthy hearts within her curriculum, involves students in the planning, and invites older students and parents to help monitor the event. The positive outcomes include making a sizable donation to the American Heart Association, earning free physical education equipment for the school from participating companies, and individual students earning prizes for their efforts. Most importantly, students make personal reflections relative to their contributions and their understanding of healthy hearts. The entire initiative honors the straightforward message of the

American Heart Association: Eat right, get moving, and live to-
bacco free.

Tree Hugger and Friends

Teaching environmental science to a group of 20 boys in the
spring of their senior year might look like a recipe for disaster.
One year, the teacher countered "senioritis" with a service learning plan that kept his students engaged while learning about environmental science in a unique way. He had them write a play
that would be performed for all of the district fourth graders,
who were also studying environmental issues. The seniors
wrote a very funny play that included all the essential learning
standards for environmental science and was a big hit with the
fourth-grade students and teachers. Through their work on the
production, the seniors gained knowledge, made a contribution,
and stayed motivated right to the end.

Modern-Day Slavery

During an oral book report by a student in an eleventh-
grade English class, an argument arose about whether modern-
day slavery really existed. Sensing strong interest in this topic,
the teacher suggested that the class develop a service learning
initiative around it. Students went on to create a very ambitious
unit that led to an all-school awareness assembly, a special
mural depicting the need for action to address this issue, and a
community-wide fundraising initiative that raised enough
money to free one slave in a Third World country.

Middle School Gender Project

Junior and senior students in an English elective course,
Women in Literature, sponsored a retreat for eighth-grade girls
attending our district middle school. Based on their readings
about strong female role models, they prepared an inspirational
program to help younger students deal with the pressures of
transitioning into high school. Issues affecting young girls, such
as relationships, media stereotypes, eating disorders, and peer
pressure, were discussed openly with older students serving as
mentors. This particular project was originally developed by a

junior girl who had heard of a similar undertaking at another school.

The projects and programs described above have several traits in common. They all involved a strong component of student voice, and each led to high levels of student enthusiasm. In schools where service learning has taken hold, the growth has been impressive. In the schools cited above, we created a mini-grant protocol, which rewarded teachers with a $100 honorarium for adopting the service learning model. The amount of money was minimal compared to the work they put in, but the incentive seemed to capture their attention. The power of service learning did the rest—teachers and students alike marveled at the enthusiasm it brought to the classroom.

Student-Directed Programs and Events

Information about student-directed programs could fill its own book. Here, I will simply highlight two programs that have had significant impact in schools where I have worked.

About six years ago, I invited student leaders at Leavitt Area High School to attend a special showing of a documentary entitled *Surviving High School*, produced by Arnold Shapiro for the Teen Files series from AIMS Multimedia. The program featured frank information about issues that affect the daily lives of teens, from suicide to anorexia to bullying, and highlighted the Challenge Day program founded by Rich and Yvonne St. John-Dutra. The video captured the imagination of the 26 students who had accepted my invitation. They made up their minds to plan a similar program.

The outcome, a four-hour student awareness program called Challenge Nite, typically accommodates as many as one hundred students, in groups of eight. The evening begins with ice-breaker activities followed by some data collection around norms that relate to school climate. After a pizza feed, the participants view *Surviving High School*. The show always moves our students emotionally, and they return to their groups eager to respond to its central themes. In their groups, facilitated by a trained student leader, they discuss various scenarios applicable to their life at school. Each group creates a poster representing their views on Challenge Nite. Toward the end of the program, students have an opportunity for emotional introspection about how they are treated and how they treat others. This activity closes with students pledging to improve relationships in their school. The evening ends with an open microphone segment in which people can come to the front of the group and share ideas or challenge others to take positive actions.

The next day, participants come to school wearing bright orange Challenge Nite t-shirts. Posters about positive connections between students decorate the halls, and orange testimonial cards plastered on the main bulletin board give great feedback on Challenge Nite. The school climate gets an immediate boost, and a buzz begins about when the next event will occur. In my experience with ten Challenge Nite programs in two schools, the success really comes from empowering students to improve their school environment. I would much rather conduct a student-delivered activity like this than hire more security to address increases in bullying or harassment.

Another excellent example of student voice in action is a program that calls on high school students to facilitate groups in Drug and Alcohol Awareness activities in a middle school. Each of my sons had this opportunity on several occasions during their high school years. Each shared with me how repeated facilitation of these groups helped them to finally grasp the information involved. They honestly doubted that the middle school age students would be able to fully understand the material, but—after two or three exposures—they thought they were finally "getting it" themselves. This may be a classic case of the teachers becoming the real learners.

Yet another student-directed program that I have had the opportunity to repeat at five or six different schools is a Teen Issues Day. (Actually, the schools have implemented several variations of these student-directed days, but Teen Issues is perhaps the easiest to describe.) On the day of the event, teachers and students come to school as always, but regular academic classes are suspended. Instead of attending English, math, or physical education classes, students participate in workshops on topics that interest them—usually three hour-long workshops, selected from a list of forty or fifty possibilities, which in turn were gleaned from a much longer list on the basis of student survey responses. For example, one student might choose a seminar on women's self-defense, a class on nutrition for peak performance, and a session on the issue of date rape; another might opt for an workshop on meditation, a yoga class, and a seminar on resisting peer pressure; a third might explore gender stereotypes, discuss curfews with the town police chief, and participate in an exercise simulating the effects of alcohol on coordination and balance.

These student-directed days are a big deal, and the bulk of the logistical work falls on the students. They conduct the surveys to determine interest, phone prospective presenters, send out confirmations, and hand-schedule their classmates based on their priority choices. Finding three slots for each of 850 students is about as much work as scheduling the school for an entire semester of classes, yet we go to all this trouble for just one day. The fact that students do so much of the work gives them an investment and ownership that cannot be duplicated in their normal school program. Teachers are relegated to supervisory roles, and they genuinely enjoy seeing the students rise to the occasion with such dedication and enthusiasm.

Each time one of these days draws to a close, we receive positive feedback from participants, teachers, and community members. Workshop evaluations reveal high levels of student learning and enjoyment. The outside presenters rave about our respectful student body and the organizational skills of our student leaders. The topics we grappled with touch our school for days and weeks to come. School climate is enhanced not only by what we learned, but how we learned it. At day's end, all the organizers are dead tired, but all insist that we should do this again—it was the best day ever!

Experiential Learning

Educational programs that offer "experiential learning" go by many names—place-based learning, senior seminar, apprenticeships, and others. Though each program has some unique components, they typically share these features: They are more student-directed than teacher-directed, they take place off campus rather than on school grounds, and they involve a more complex situation than the typical high school for-credit offering.

Perhaps the most inspiring element of experiential learning is the inherent level of student autonomy it allows. The student selects the experience, determines its processes, plans the learning, prepares an exhibition, and finally attempts to convince a review panel that the work has value. The following examples illustrate how this unfolds.

One of my first experiences with the notion of experiential learning came nearly a decade ago. As a high school principal, I recruited ten seniors out of a study hall to develop a protocol for a senior seminar concluding with a student exhibition. My timing wasn't great; it's tough to get seniors to do something extra during their last semester of high school. But the effort did yield a few shining moments that drove stronger efforts in subsequent years.

The highlight had to be the work of a girl I'll call Kat. A good student, though not one who easily conformed to institutional expectations, Kat had her own voice, her own pace; her substantial skills took her much farther than her commitment. For her senior seminar topic, she chose fashion design. Kat had really connected with the teacher of a Fiber and Fabric course, who agreed to serve as her mentor. Kat caught fire as a student that spring, plunging into the retail and design aspects of the fashion industry. She designed a knitted hat that she eventually placed in shops in a neighboring city. For her final exhibition, she put on a fashion show at our school, with her classmates wearing her designs. Embracing experiential learning with courage and ingenuity, Kat turned her "senior slide" into "senior soar."

Another early success story involved a senior I'll call Megan, who approached me needing a couple of extra credits to fill her second semester schedule. When I asked about possible career interests, she said that she might want to teach at the elementary school level. Within minutes, we had devised a way for her to assist in a third-grade classroom for a couple hours each day. Working with a high school English teacher who served as her mentor, she identified some supplemental reading—a book about teaching youngsters how to read and a novel about the life of a teacher. Megan also kept a daily journal and prepared an exit exhibition about her experiences as they related to our state learning standards.

Speaking to a review committee of four teachers and several eleventh-grade students, Megan gave a very thoughtful and introspective evaluation of her work. She spoke of finding the balance between being friendly with third graders and maintaining discipline. She described the difficulty of teaching students with disabilities. She discussed the value of planning and the need to be ready to adjust. In short, her exhibition hit the high notes of a university-level teacher preparation syllabus. Megan had been looking for a filler to complete her last semester of high school; instead, she designed and participated in the richest learning experience of her life. She knew what her future career felt like, and she knew what she had to do to become good at it.

One summer, I met with a boy I'll call Alex. After three years at a private high school, he and his parents were exploring other options. Alex was an excellent student, bent on an engineering career and hoping to attend a technical institute following graduation. He sought some hands-on experiences that did not seem to be possible at his very traditional private school. He still needed to take calculus, physics, and a few other requirements, but those would hardly fill his schedule, and he had little interest in the other courses offered for seniors there or at Kennebunk High School. When I started describing an experiential learning option, I could tell that they were sold.

At the time, KHS followed an alternating block schedule, with four 80-minute classes on Blue Days and four different classes on White Days. Alex came to school on Blue Days and one period on White Days. The rest of the time was set aside for experiential learning. With one of our industrial technology teachers as a mentor, he ventured into the community looking for meaningful learning. Several days later, he outlined, and I approved, a plan that included a one-credit independent study with his industrial technology mentor and a two-credit sequence in the community.

Alex spent the first nine weeks of his senior year shadowing a community entrepreneur—a man in his seventies who had rich insights and know-how to share with a high school trainee. During the second nine weeks, Alex apprenticed with a local company, helping them with website marketing, promotion, and other facets of their building inspection business. Bolstered by these experiences, he spent the final semester embarking on his own business. Taking orders over the Internet, he bored out manifolds on automobile engines to increase their horsepower. I had little understanding of the mechanical aspects of engine manifolds or why anyone would need such a service, but Alex had plenty of work orders. At year's end, he successfully presented his project to a review committee of seven teachers. He left KHS more than ready to enter one of the technical institutes. Our "school for each kid" had worked for Alex.

It also worked for a girl I'll call Claudine, a top student and a bit of a nonconformist. Claudine had approached her guidance counselor during the spring of junior year and asked about spending a semester abroad, but not in a formal program: She simply wanted to travel, earning her way by working in the communities where she stayed. We readily agreed to support her time away from us as part of our experiential learning program.

Claudine worked independently with several of our teachers while she traveled. For example, she kept a daily journal and wrote articles for our school newspaper as a foreign correspondent, earning part of an English credit. We made similar special arrangements for work in math and art, but essentially the travel experience itself was her curriculum.

In the performance exhibition she gave upon her return, Claudine wove together personal reflections from the perspective of literature and history in a presentation that would rival a course syllabus in either area. She drew contextual connections about life, family, travel, and growing up that were both intelligent and perceptive. As a seventeen-year-old traveling on her own, she was truly in charge of her day-to-day existence.

School-sponsored community service, service learning, student-directed events, and experiential learning bring the world into our classrooms and our students into the world. When we honor our students' voices, respect their abilities, and allow them to choose their own paths, we set them on a journey that can last a lifetime.

5

Showcasing Talents, Building Skills

Students engaged in athletic activities, drama programs, academic clubs, musical organizations, and other extra- and co-curricular activities encounter rich opportunities for learning and leadership. Schools that set out to promote student voice may find it easiest to start in this arena. In fact, my work as a coach probably provided me with my first glimpse of the power of student voice.

Coaching a struggling basketball team through a long losing streak, I kept upping the ante, placing more demands and more controls on our game plan. The harder I tried, the worse the team played. After one scrimmage, I flat-out accused them of laziness and lack of pride. I went home convinced that my tongue-lashing would inspire them to get their act together. But that very evening, my senior captains paid a visit to my home. Diplomatically, even graciously, these two young men challenged my assertions that they were not trying hard enough. In fact, they said, the players were wound up tighter than tight because of my attempts to control the game.

I listened hard that night. Over time, I learned that if I gave my players some input into decisions, they gradually took more ownership. Running plays and executing game plans that they helped develop, they played with greater spirit. With inspiration came success; with success came respect; with respect came a willingness to commit to more demanding program goals.

My teams didn't win any world championships, but we were finally able to compete. The lessons I learned about the power of student voice in the athletic arena indisputably transfer to a wider school setting. Giving students a voice in school is no different than having basketball players help you devise an out-of-bounds play. Even if the play isn't up to professional standards, they're more likely to execute it successfully if they own it. And success can provide the impetus to raise expectations.

One natural avenue for student voice in sports programs and activities is the leadership opportunities they provide. This goes beyond the longstanding tradition of electing or appointing team captains or club officers. I remember watching drama club students rehearse for *The Music Man*. With more than forty students on stage, the director set out to block a large production number. I knew from experience that the results would be polished and professional. What impressed me, though, was the way the director tapped into student voice to get there. With skill and enthusiasm, he led students to make suggestions, refine their work, and pull it all together in a complex and spirited performance.

Likewise, Kennebunk High School's fledgling dance team offered student voice an opportunity to blossom. The advisor encouraged students to collaborate in choreographing and refining the pieces they would perform. In just two years, the dancers began to incorporate more difficult moves and execute them with greater skill. In particular, two girls who had not found a niche in school stepped forward and become real leaders. Their increased confidence, assertiveness, and self-esteem were every bit as exhilarating as their performance.

Co-curricular programs and activities offer many such occasions for student ownership and leadership. When they showcase student skills, they create opportunities for recognition that in turn enhances motivation. Though such engaging opportunities can be hard to replicate within the regular curriculum, we can learn much about what works with young people from these programs.

Spotlight on Students

Showcasing student skills is one of the best and most common ways to give students a voice. Student performance, whether athletic, academic, or artistic, is fundamentally a form of voice. Much as the talented singer takes center stage in a school's musical production, strong science students exhibit their skills at the annual science fair. When we offer students such opportunities in a multitude of settings, we honor who they are, giving them a voice through their talents and interests.

Schools can never do enough in this regard. Here again, educators can learn a great deal from the athletic arena. Spurred by the incentive of public performance, many a youngster has learned perseverance, patience, and discipline on the baseball diamond, basketball court, or gymnastics mat. Schools can take advantage of the same incentive with reading, writing, and arithmetic. Coffeehouses and Poetry Nights honor students' writing skills. Student film festivals, art exhibits, and songwriting competitions promote their artistic talents. Such programs put student skills, interests, and passions in the public eye and provide a wider audience for student work.

The dance team at Kennebunk High School grew from a seed planted during just such an exhibition. The dance teacher asked our student council to allow a small group of students from her dance classes to perform a number during the school's Spirit Week assembly. The student council obliged, and the dance students performed a basic dance number that was memorable mostly because it got the students noticed. Just two years later, the dance team was performing for sellout audiences. Dance team members had developed their own identity, their own voice.

The math team, the art club, the French club, the wrestlers, the knitters, and the students who excel at woodworking all deserve such attention. Showcasing their performances brings meaning to their passion, and that meaning inspires continued improvement.

Special Student Clubs

Extra- and co-curricular offerings provide valuable opportunities for student voice across a broad spectrum of activities. Here we focus on school clubs whose mission statements explicitly incorporate student voice, extending the notions of democracy and citizenship to a level not generally found in other clubs. Examples of such organizations, and stories that relate to them, follow.

Peer Mediators

In this club, a group of students are trained in conflict resolution skills and work within the school when disputes arise. My first exposure to peer mediation occurred at a high school that had endured a rash of fights. That year, we sent a group of students to an overnight leadership conference. They returned home with an action plan to help reduce fighting. One of the initiatives was a peer mediation group that would seek to resolve disputes between students before a fistfight broke out.

During the year that we developed the peer mediation program, 37 fights had erupted. After we launched the program, the number shrank to a half dozen. Subsequent years saw a further decrease in fighting. In a typical year, our peer mediators would intervene in a couple of dozen disputes and successfully resolve the vast majority of them. The assistant principal found the program a boon. In the past, despite his efforts to resolve these student conflicts, they usually simmered or escalated until he had to deal with a serious disciplinary issue.

Student mediators are trained to take the two people in conflict and help them find nonviolent solutions to the issues that confront them. When teachers, administrators, or students hear of a conflict brewing, they refer the students involved to peer mediation. Referred students have a choice about participating, but they typically do, for the alternative is usually administrative intervention and disciplinary procedures. Once the parties have agreed to enter into mediation, two peer mediators are selected to facilitate the meeting. The only adult involved is the peer mediation team advisor, who stands by in case the mediation should break down. The goal is to have both parties leave the meeting with a plan to end the conflict. Because most conflicts factor down to misunderstandings and misinformation, just getting two students in a safe environment where they are able to communicate their feelings generally heads them towards lasting solutions.

This organization has powerful implications for student voice. At the ground floor, the students in conflict are able to use their voices in constructive conversation, rather than the destructive rumor mill that typically escalates such conflicts. The peer mediators use their voices to assist their school in establishing a safe and orderly climate. Adults trust them to bring a levelheaded approach and peaceful solutions to volatile situations. Throughout the process, students are empowered to find answers without adult intervention. In the best outcome of all, student mediators learn conflict resolution skills that will last a lifetime. Students in the school get a sense that disputes can be settled through solid communication. All of this represents student voice at its best.

One of my favorite recollections of this initiative goes back to an incident in the program's fourth year. By then, fights in our school were a rarity. But during a Friday night football game, an ugly confrontation erupted between one of our ninth graders and a teen who didn't attend our school. A crowd soon gathered, but the police officers on duty intervened, quickly restoring order. Following the game, I was chaperoning a dance in our cafeteria. As I stood at the door greeting our kids, I heard one expression of regret after another. Students were visibly disappointed that this had happened at their school—a place where they had worked so hard to wipe out fighting.

Civil Rights Team

In reaction to the tragedy at Columbine High School, the racial and ethnic tensions that affected schools in the mid-1990s, and the growing concerns about harassment, schools in Maine have been encouraged to form civil rights teams. At the last two schools where I have worked, very active teams work closely with the state attorney general's office in promoting tolerance.

Both of these schools had little racial diversity, but the team found many areas where their work was needed. I recall one student making a presentation about the civil rights team at our school during a workshop on student voice in Seattle. An audience member from an urban school asked Katie whether we had racial diversity in our school. To me, the question seemed to imply that the efforts of our civil rights team would falter in a racially charged setting. Katie offered a powerful retort. "There is more than one kind of diversity, and in our school it plays out in socioeconomic ways." She went on to talk about other tensions affecting our students, from religious differences to sexual orientation. Her decisive answer won applause from the 50 or 60 attendees.

Our civil right teams are trained in the legal aspects of racial slurs, hate crimes, harassment, and bullying. They are charged with reporting incidents of such unwanted behaviors to the school administration. Although the public perception of their mission may stop there, in reality their work lies much more in the marketing end of civil rights. The teams sponsor projects that encourage tolerance and honor diversity within our school. For example, they have promoted civil rights discussions during Black History Week and spearheaded the school-wide production of *The Laramie Project*, a play about a hate crime.

These students are encouraged to speak out against injustice, practice good citizenship, and influence their peers to do the same. Their grassroots involvement goes a long way toward helping schools manage important societal issues appropriately.

D.A.R.T. Team

The D.A.R.T. team has been a fixture at Kennebunk High School since the early 1980s. Initially, the acronym stood for Drug and Alcohol Rehabilitation Team—part of a statewide movement for municipalities to form school and community teams that would work to address concerns about drug and alcohol use and abuse by young people. Teams brought together students, teachers, town officials, and citizens at large. Twenty-five years later, this membership configuration remains intact, with nearly equal numbers of students, teachers, and senior citizens.

However, the scope of the committee's work has changed dramatically. The team once focused on identifying young people with drug and alcohol problems and getting them treatment. As prevention of drug and alcohol abuse grew in importance, the D.A.R.T. team adjusted its role. Today D.A.R.T. stands for Developing Assets and Responsibilities Together. The teams now focus on helping young people in our communities develop assets that support good decision-making about high-risk behaviors, including the use of illegal substances. Their work is guided, in part, by the literature regarding the Forty Developmental Assets put forth by the Search Institute.[13]

The work of the D.A.R.T. team now only brushes slightly into the realm of alcohol use and abuse. One recent initiative, for example, focused on promoting quality family time. Through "Take a Break Night," the D.A.R.T. team encouraged families to pause in the hustle and bustle of daily living for just one evening at home as a family unit. Team members spoke at local elementary schools, the Rotary Club, and other organizations to build enthusiasm for the project.

In another recent project, the D.A.R.T. team hosted a series of discussion nights on various teen issues. Coming together in a "town meeting" format, adults and students talked about topics such as the relationship between youth and law enforcement in our communities, the effect of peer pressure on teens, and stress in the lives of high school students.

By bringing senior citizens and youth together to work through common concerns, the D.A.R.T. process leads to communication, respect, modeling, and a host of other positive outcomes.

KHS Connections

A girl I'll call Diane came into my office one day with an idea to improve the transition process for ninth graders entering our school. At breakneck speed, she rattled off a plan to create a mentoring program where high school juniors would meet with eighth graders. In the next school year, the seniors would serve as big brothers or sisters to the new ninth graders.

---

[13] See www.searchinstitute.org/assets/forty.html, accessed July 28, 2005.

When I finally got a word in edgewise, I was able to say, "Diane, you have such great ideas!"

A month or so later, we were busing 40 eleventh-grade participants to the middle school to meet with their eighth-grade counterparts. Not surprisingly, Diane ran the whole show, with handouts, activities and discussion questions ready to go.

Three years later, Diane's idea is still very much part of the eighth-to-ninth-grade transition. The KHS Connections group helps school leaders with parent orientation and scheduling nights, and they also give up a day of their summer break to help with our ninth-grade orientation.

Within this program, student voice really thrives. *Students* answer questions from the concerned parents of eighth graders. *Students* explain the lay of the land at Kennebunk High School to incoming students. From the outset of their experience with us, the newcomers and their families see that students belong here; this is their school. Our older students take pride in adopting the younger students and mentoring them to success. Of course, Diane's great idea and strong voice made this all possible.

Peer Helpers

Another longstanding organization at Kennebunk High School is the Peer Helpers club. The name speaks for itself: The group's primary function is to help other students in a variety of ways, from tutoring to having new students "shadow" old-timers.

As one of their annual projects, Peer Helpers put together a handbook for entering students that is written from a student's point of view. Unlike the typical student handbook prepared by school administrators, it covers material that adults would not think of including: how to get a lunch ticket, where to hang out before school, how to make a phone call. Some of the items are a bit humorous, but the handbook also includes great tips about study skills, organization, and school success.

Like most of the groups mentioned in this section, the Peer Helpers group got a real boost as student voice started to emerge at our school. Now, its members take advantage of one opportunity after another to make a difference. In the latest project,

Wellness Day, regular classes were suspended while students attended workshops in areas of interest to them.

And Many More

Other school organizations that deserve mention in this section include service clubs, such as Key Clubs or Interact Clubs—student organizations comparable to adult clubs such as Kiwanis, Rotary, or Jaycees. Much like their adult counterparts, these student groups can play a huge role in the fabric of a school or community. Many schools also have debate teams, mock trial teams, model state legislatures, or political affairs clubs. These political organizations will be discussed in a later chapter of this book.

Schools across the country offer many other student organizations that serve the school community. Some schools have student disciplinary review panels or judiciary committees; others have academic honesty committees or curriculum review boards. As we have seen, almost any aspect of school can tap into student voice. The examples cited here are but the tip of the iceberg.

Student Publications

Any review of the literature on student voice yields a wealth of material related to student publications, and specifically to student newspapers. In the eyes of many, student voice begins and ends with the fact that the First Amendment protection for freedom of the press applies to student publications. As we have seen, student voice extends to a much wider arena, but the concept of press freedom for students is immensely important. Student publications can indeed be two-edged swords, representing the best and the worst of student voice.

Many years ago, I was an assistant principal in a high school that had a rather controversial school newspaper. Although the principal had the final word on what was published, my son happened to be the paper's editor; as a result, I received a great deal of on-the-job training in the art of censorship. The newspaper crew was a witty bunch, and most articles contained at least one sentence or paragraph that had me roaring with laughter. However, sometimes their humor crossed boundaries and forced either the newspaper advisor or the principal to step in and require some editing. During the two years that my son served as editor, I got in on all this fun. If memory serves me correctly, there were only a few contentious situations; evidently the advisor, the principal, and my son and I did okay.

The local university sponsored an annual high school journalism conference, and the conference organizers always encouraged our school to attend. We had perhaps the freest above-ground student publication in the state, and they loved using us as an example of free press. I was sometimes embarrassed by the attention our publication received—just crossing my fingers that school leaders were not too lenient about the paper's content.

A decade later, I am the principal of a First Amendment Schools project school, and our school newspaper was a major factor in earning that national distinction. We have a wonderful school newspaper, with an excellent advisor and effective operating procedures. I don't worry about whether I censor the paper properly, because in actuality I don't censor it at all! Over the course of two years and some twenty issues, I have made two or three minor suggestions to the student editors. These have not been seen as censorship, but rather as suggestions that promote the paper's continued success. Perhaps we have been lucky to avoid controversy for so long, but fortune smiles on those who are prepared.

The advisor, Molly Pierce, knows that her journalism class would disintegrate if censorship issues became commonplace, so she has done a great job at gatekeeping. Her students, who love their involvement with this class, are careful not to jeopardize its status in our school and community. They understand full well that rights, freedoms and privileges carry with them responsibilities, and they accept ownership of the appropriateness of their work. Included here is a brief set of standards that the newspaper staff at Kennebunk High School works from and an explanation of the point (grading) system. As with so many protocols used in education, this has benefited from a number of authors; Molly Pierce adapted parts of this from the work of Carrisa Crozier at Arapahoe High School in Littleton, CO. While the grading system might not be as important at a school where a club rather than a class puts out the paper, it certainly illustrates the complexity of the tasks involved!

Newspaper Guidelines
2004–2005

Staff set-up: In this student-directed class, student editors lead staffs, edit stories for content and fact checking/ethical soundness, layout pages, and produce the end product. The breakdown of editors includes the chief, current events or news editor, feature, sports, and photo editors, as well as a business manager. The advisor oversees and "advises" all staffers and editors to correct story format, interviewing, and design, as well as understanding of ethical and legal background, brainstorming ideas, PageMaker comprehension, and all other journalistic necessities.

Stories: Staffers choose their ideas and are expected to work on every story until it is deemed "excellent" by their peers and by the teacher.

This includes a breakdown of three deadlines per issue: Deadline #1 includes the initial story idea (slug), one interview, and interview notes. Deadline #2 is a printout of the BEST story possible, including at least three interviews and credible facts that have been checked for accuracy, and the third deadline is finished story, having been edited by student editor and corrections made, saved on desktop and ready for layout onto PageMaker program.

After approval and before printing, stories and layout are looked over (prior reviewed) by administration for any red flags.

Deadlines: Real journalists work under strict deadlines. If their stories are not completed by a certain time, those stories do not get into the paper. Students are expected to adhere to the deadlines that are set for each story worked on.

(cont'd.)

Class set-up: I believe this class is the most "true to life" class a student is able to take in his or her high school career. Along with being responsible for his or her own grade, he or she is also responsible for the staff as a whole; if one story is missed, an entire staff must pick up the pieces and problem-solve to correct the situation, all while working within a strict deadline system. But there is much freedom and FUN involved as well, and I believe each student on staff would tell you this.

For each class, students are expected to log all work done that block and outside of class and are also expected to keep track of POINTS earned during that block as well. (See POINTS sheet for specific breakdown of points earned.) All students are able to, and most do, achieve an A upon acceptance into this advanced English elective.

All staffers are also expected to sell at least one AD per semester, as each issue costs a few hundred dollars to produce. Subscriptions are also available through the advisor or the business manager for $10 per year.

Ramblings Point Sheets
2004–2005

On the following pages are listings for the various jobs and assignments for students on newspaper staff. Refer to this listing when collecting materials for your weekly files.

Every **Monday** or **Tuesday** (depending on the week), each newspaper staff member is to turn in his/her file for Mrs. Pierce. In each file should be the following items:

1. Weekly Point Sheet filled out as completely as possible. **If this sheet is not complete, or clips are missing, points will NOT be awarded.** If cheating is discovered on the Points Sheet, ALL points for the week will be nullified.
2. **All dates & times, clips, articles, forms, etc., are needed to verify each claim for points.** Be thorough to ensure credit for claimed points.

The file will be checked and the weekly total given. The point file comprises the entire grade in newspaper. Grade scale is as follows:

First Quarter:
- 1000 points and above = A
- 999–825 points = B
- 824–725 points = C
- 724–600 points = D
- < 600 points = F

Second Quarter:
- 1200 points and above = A
- 1119–935 points = B
- 934–815 points = C
- 814–725 points = D
- < 724 points = F

Semester Totals:

- 3400 and above = A
- 3399–2720 = B
- 1719–1375 = C
- 1274–2000 = D
- < 2000 = F

Additional requirements for an A per semester:

- min. $\frac{1}{16}$ page ad OR 3 contact tries (1 pt/$ sold)
- proof of 4 article types published (100 points)
- reading assignments
- shadow an editor to learn PageMaker
- photograph for a story (30 pts/photo)

Story Approval Steps:

1. Complete slug sheet and conduct first interview. Bring notes and map to Deadline #1 and get story dated.

2. Complete rest of interviews and type story. Save story to appropriate disk. Make sure story has a complete header. Get story read and signed by primary source. Bring story printout (with map and notes attached to back) to Deadline #2.

3. Story must be peer edited by your section editor and the editor-in-chief. Make their corrections and bring a new printout to Deadline #3A. Mrs. Pierce will read and edit the story. If a second reading is necessary, you will be scheduled for Deadline #3B.

4. Make requested corrections, additions, and improvements and provide a new printout for Deadline #3B or—if no Deadline #3B is requested—for Deadline #4.

5. Editor-in-chief or section editor will give the story its final approval . . . Deadline #4.

(cont'd.)

Making up a story or quotes for a story (not counting the April Fool's Issue) will result in the semester grade being lowered one letter at the end of the semester. A second occurrence will result in the student being dropped from the class.

Points for each of the tasks of newspaper publication are outlined on the following pages. **Only work completed ON TIME will be ELIGIBLE FOR POINTS.**

Work on any story/page may be shared with another student. If work is shared, a teamwork form must be submitted so that points may be distributed correctly. Point values for the task do not double and students must decide how to divide the possible point value.

<u>Point Folders</u> (all staff)
20 points for weekly point folder in on time (Monday or Tuesday of each week). NOTE: Unless a student is absent from school, no point folders will be accepted later than **one day after the assigned day** of each week and points earned that week will NOT be counted.

These points may **only be claimed if you have done work** for the paper during the week. You must have had a story dated, edited someone's work, worked on a graph, etc. Work claimed must be documented with dates on weekly points sheets, signatures on edits, or work in progress included in folder. Claiming only "time" will not qualify as documented work.

<u>Attendance</u> (all staff)
15 points per hour for supervised after-hours work on *Ramblings*. Working during a FULL lunch period is 15 points. A full unscheduled hour is also worth 15 points. At least 30 minutes of an hour counts as 5 points, less is no points. **Date and time <u>must</u> be listed along with work done during this time period. (Date + Time + Task)**

Time will not be credited if other documented work is not also included on the point folder. That is, you may not claim "time only."

Time spent finishing a deadline after the deadline has passed will not earn points.

A maximum of 75 points may be claimed for after-hours work on any given day.

–20 points for a tardy.

–50 points for an unexcused absence or abuse of the hall pass privilege.

<u>Copy Writing</u> (all staff)
Each staff member must write a minimum of two story assignments each paper.

Each staff member must write at least one of each story type (news, sports, editorial/critical review, feature/in-depth) during the semester.

Up to 30 points for meeting each of the Deadlines #1–3 (10 pts/story if ALL are ready)

50 points if all stories meet Deadline #4 (Layout Deadline)

5 points per column inch for published story (up to 50 points). (Attach printout)

3 points per column inch for unpublished story (up to 30 points). (Attach printout)

Up to 60 points for story evaluation (a holistic grade, a number from 1–6, will be assigned each story by Mrs. Pierce at Deadline #3A; multiply this number by 10 for the evaluation value).

100 points for proof of writing each of the story types during the semester. Submit labeled clips of the stories in the final point folder of the semester.

<u>Proofing/Editing</u>
Section editors/Editor-in-chief: 5 points per story edited (signature and comments must appear on story printout)

Reporters: 25 points for editing designed page (must autograph and sign proofing list)

<u>Headlines</u>
10 points per flush left or kicker headline published (clip) (may be claimed by ONE person)

10 points for unique headline published (clip) (may be shared; use Teamwork form)

5 points for standing headlines rerun in subsequent newspaper

(cont'd.)

<u>Art & Graphics</u> (all staff)

50 points per published stand-alone cartoon done by Deadline #3A (clip)

30 points for story illustration done by Deadline #3A (clip)

20 points per unpublished but requested art (attach) Max. of 40 points per issue.

20 points per published chart or graph done by Deadline #3A (clip)

50 points for published creative graph or chart (graph contains art to aid the communication)

25 points for list, Q & A box, map, etc.

5 points for standing art re-run in subsequent newspaper

<u>Photography</u> (all staff)

30 points per published picture done by Deadline #3A (Max. 120 points per issue). Not including headshot pictures.

15 points per athletic event shot and published (clip)

5 points per scanned/adjusted photo (may also add time spent outside of class) (clip)

10 points for photo brought in from outside staff (obtained from club member, etc.) (clip)

<u>Design</u> (all staff)

30 points per dummy page layout (planned on mini-layout before computer design begins).

(If more than one person did the page, decide how much credit each receives and include Teamwork forms in point folders.)

100 points per page layout done on computer on time and ready for staff proofing. (When more than one person works on the page, decide how to divide the credit. Include Teamwork forms.)

30 points per page layout done after proofing deadline (date and time specified).

0 points for page layout if the page holds up the publication and the printer deadline has to be changed.

Up to 25 **bonus** points per page layout for creative grid design

–25 points per edit missing on final page design (subtracted from page designer & editing crew)

–10 points for each error that goes to press (subtracted from page designer & editing crew)

Circulation (all staff)

1 point per dollar for ads sold (clip and include in point folder after ad is published; payment must be collected before ad credit [points] can be given)

5 points per business contacted for ads (attach business contact sheet, which must be filled out completely, including response from business). Maximum of 10 businesses per week

40 points per ad designed (clip and include in point folder)

25 points for mailing ad invoices for an issue (job of ad manager)

25 points per subscription sold (attach subscription contact sheet, which must be filled out completely)

25 points per ½ hour spent in preparing, folding, and mailing subscriptions out

10 points per school distribution (maximum 3 times per semester)

Fundraising (all staff)

10 points for brainstorming an event that actually happens

30 points for each hour helping with a fundraising event

½ point for each dollar raised in total of event (must be present at event to get points)

Other Activities (all staff)

50 points for taking Mrs. Pierce along on an interview and getting an interview critique (maximum of 1 per six weeks)

10 points for getting an interview critique sheet filled out by a person you interviewed (one/story)

50 points per reading assignment made by instructor. Attach a summary of the article/reading assignment and indicate how you will use the information (if you don't write the summary, you must take a test on the material). At least one reading will be assigned each 6-week grading period.

25 points per independent reading assignment—maximum of 2 per six weeks. Get prior approval of reading material. Attach a summary and indicate how you will use the information.

15 points per clipped graphic idea with explanation of how you will use the idea on your page

20 points for incorporating the idea into your page design

(cont'd.)

All conferences must be either school sponsored or preapproved for points to be earned. Include all notes and handouts to receive credit for any of these conference options. If conference includes a contest, no points will be awarded until the contest entry is completed and submitted.

75 points for attendance at fall or spring conference, or other one-day workshop (include handouts, notes, etc.). Write a one-page summary/evaluation of the conference.

50 points for attendance at off-campus press conference arranged through the school.

50 points for submitting writing to another publication, including *The Rambler* yearbook.

30 points for photo contributed to *The Rambler*.

50 points for story or photo submitted to professional press (maximum of 1 each 6 weeks)

25 **bonus** points if story or photo is printed in professional press

20 points per entry in contest (maximum of 100 points per semester)

25 **bonus** points if entry wins contest

50 points for special project (maximum of 1 per 6 weeks); projects must receive prior advisor approval and be completed before the beginning of the last week of any grading period.

Possible Beats:

KHS Clubs	Government
Performing Arts (theater, band, choir)	Health
	KHS (specific) sports
Visual Arts (photo, art, jewelry)	Lifestyle
	Medicine
Business	Minorities
Computers/Internet	News
Crime	Politics
Diversity	Religion
Drugs	Science
Education	Technology
Fashion	Weather
Foreign affairs	Women's Issues

As the principal, I also play an important role in this school newspaper's success. I must constantly remind myself of the importance of letting students have a voice and trusting that they will use their freedom wisely. My attitude as I read their work has to be to find the good, rather than find the bad. I hold fast to the idea that I do not want individuals hurt or embarrassed by the newspaper's content. Students for the most part understand this, just as they understand our need to protect others. Ultimately, however, if something hurtful did appear in the paper—well, we'd just have to take steps to repair the damage and move forward. It's unrealistic to expect that something as potentially fickle as media coverage will never lead to some negativity, so we deal with it the best we can.

Student publications in all forms can create testy situations. Yearbooks and literary publications are other examples of initiatives that need administrative attention. Like the student newspaper, these are rich illustrations of student voice that become very public. Students and advisors need to know from the outset what limitations exist and how these varied publications can be developed in a positive way. Perhaps that is the key point: Student publications are inherently positive; students will deliver according to our expectations.

6

Educating for Citizenship

Citizenship Matters

On December 5, 2004, the Honorable Lee Hamilton delivered the keynote address[14] at the second Congressional Conference on Civic Education in Washington, D.C. Director of the Woodrow Wilson International Center for Scholars, Hamilton represented Indiana in Congress for 34 years and was vice chairman of the National Commission on Terrorist Attacks upon the United States (known as the 9/11 Commission). The following synopsis of his address will serve as a springboard to a discussion about the civic mission of schools—to teach, prepare, and inspire young people to become engaged citizens.

Hamilton began by remembering the September 11, 2001, attacks on America and the questions they invoke for Americans. He asked, "What are we defending when we defend America, and what does it mean, individually, to be part of America?" He answered his own questions by stating that we are really defending our beliefs—beliefs such as "that we are one nation indivisible, that representative democracy is the best form of government, and that with freedoms come obligations."

---

[14] © 2004 by the Education Commission of the States (ECS).

He then challenged us to defend our nation by honoring and teaching these cherished ideas. "We need to learn and teach the techniques of a healthy democracy—participation, consensus building, compromise, civility and rational discourse." He called for us to strengthen this effort in our schools and all of our institutions. He called for an expansion of the dialogue of democracy, and cautioned us about the dangerous ground on which dialogue in our country currently stands. "We need to keep an eye on the target—which is to resolve differences and reconcile views, not to exacerbate differences and demonize opposing views."

Hamilton concluded his address by indicating that being an American provides us an opportunity for greatness—an opportunity to teach our students of their chance and their responsibility to be part of a new birth of freedom.

This stirring address provides schools with a call to action that validates the notion of getting students civically involved. We must provide them opportunities to practice the tools needed to become successful citizens.

Educating for Democracy

A close friend recently told me about a conversation with his seventeen-year-old daughter. When she asked about the topic of my second book, he explained that it was about getting students involved in their school and community and helping them learn the skills of citizenship. He used the example of the recent (2004) presidential election, to exemplify the need to get young people engaged in the process of governance. All this simply drew a blank stare from his daughter—as if to say, why would she ever vote? If young people are so disenfranchised that voting makes little sense to them, then their lack of understanding about other basic freedoms ought not to come as a shock.

Schools must accept some responsibility for this tragedy. We need to stop the decay of democratic ideals in our schools. We can turn this negative course around. We can, and must, educate a new generation of civic-minded youth.

The Civic Mission of Schools

The Civic Mission of Schools (CMS) report, published in February 2003 by the Carnegie Corporation and CIRCLE (Center for Information and Research on Civic Learning and Engagement at the University of Maryland), informs us that most American youth have little understanding of representative democracy and their role in it.[15] Suggesting that schools can play a major role in correcting this problem, the report identified six approaches to good civic education:

Instruction in government, history, law and democracy

Granted, educators these days have their plates full. It might seem overwhelming to pile on anything new. But the teaching of history, government, and law is anything but new; even our founding fathers recognized the need to educate our youth if the experiment in democracy was to succeed. Many of our schools have moved away from these basic lessons. However, as schools examine the standards that all students need to reach, these areas must be near the top of the list.

Class discussion of current local, national, and international issues and events

The opportunity for students to be emotionally involved in current issues on both a local and global scale can provide strong training in community involvement. The habits formed by having students pay attention can help minimize the apathy that exists in our nation's young adults.

Community service and service learning linked to curriculum and class instruction

We have already addressed the role that community service and service learning can play in quality educational programs. The sense of accomplishment and positive self-image that these programs promote tell only half of the story. The opportunity for student voice, academic connections, and the

---

[15] See www.civicmissionofschools.org, accessed July 28, 2005.

development of civic habits are valuable outcomes of student participation.

Extracurricular opportunities to get involved in the school and community

As redundant as it may seem, student involvement and engagement in their school and community makes everything else possible. To motivate students, we must offer them access to activities—whether athletic, artistic, academic, civic, social, or cultural—that matter to them.

Participation in school governance

Schools must demonstrate societal models of good governance. Regardless of the form and structure of school government, students should be given some say in the decisions that affect their curriculum and the school environment.

Simulations of democratic processes and procedures

What is important here is that schools should accept some responsibility for creating scenarios in which students experience voting, debating, and decision-making—scenarios that afford them opportunities to practice the skills of democracy.

Without question, these six areas of focus can provide educators with excellent opportunities to develop citizenship skills in our students. Let's look at some of these experiences in civic engagement.

Student Governance

A school organization needs a well-defined governance structure similar to that of any municipality. Involving students in that governance structure is not only a sensible idea, it is an idea that should be part of a school's responsibility—part of a school's mission.

Student government, or student council, has long been viewed as the program where this civic mission of schools was accomplished. The reality is that few schools even scratch the surface of involving students in government. To quote Dennis

Littky, "voting for the prom queen is not democracy."[16] To elevate the voice of students in our schools, we must broaden the traditional idea of student government. First and foremost, we must provide our student councils with opportunities to make real decisions that affect their schools. Let's start there.

In most schools, the work of student councils provides a degree of social leadership. Student governments organize spirit week, homecoming, winter carnival or the prom; students get to vote on themes, elect kings and queens, possibly even choose the location of the prom. Even class officers' work is essentially unremarkable: Will the class sell fruit or chocolate for their major fundraiser? All of these activities are good for students who care about the outcome of these events—but they have little to do with the educational outcomes of the school. Schools can do so much better at giving their student leaders authentic leadership opportunities.

What areas in the realm of school-based decisions need to be off limits to students? I cannot think of one. Decisions about curriculum, decisions about the school environment, even important safety considerations such as emergency lockdown procedures can benefit from student input. The first step in creating better student government is to approach school decisions with the view that students can have a say in the outcome.

Membership and participation concerns plague many student councils. Typically, students are elected to a post on student government. More often than not, these elections boil down to popularity contests that have little to do with the politics of schools. Even though some schools try to have candidates for the student council or class officers deliver speeches prior to elections, very few have programs that really involve much in the way of governing opportunities to talk about. For years, I worked in schools where—regardless of our noble intentions—the student government was made up of the most popular students. Their leadership skills or commitment to a particular

---

[16] Dennis Littky and Samantha Grabelle, Voting for homecoming queen does not prepare students for democracy. *Journal of the Coalition of Essential Schools* 21(1), 2004.

agenda had nothing to do with their appointment. If fact, some merely used the government post to bolster their college resume and rarely attended meetings.

At Kennebunk High School, we did away with student council elections two years ago. Instead, anyone who wishes a voice on the student council can become a voting member by attending three meetings. This allows those who are really passionate about leadership and making a difference to participate regardless of their place in the social order. The outcome has been surprisingly positive. In the past, the school had a 24-member council, but only about 10 members actually attended the meetings. Under the new format, 40 to 50 students show up at each meeting, and student leaders have begun to emerge.

We have some challenges around conducting meetings with so many students eager to participate, but that is a nice problem to have, and we'll sort it out in time. After all, our governing bodies at the state and national level operate with many more people. Models exist that we can learn from.

However, if the only way to bring about change is to join the student council, we are not providing all students with opportunities to participate in governance. Whether the governing body is elected or open, the issue remains: How can other students have an impact on decisions at the school? We must seek ways to make student government more inclusive. When I was principal at Leavitt Area High School, the student council followed a legislative model of government based on open sessions. Anyone in the school could write a bill. Several times a year, the student council considered new bills in an open-microphone town meeting. This format afforded every student an opportunity to weigh in on the proposed legislation. The process involved very strict guidelines about how bills were written, debated, and passed into law. There were strong checks and balances between students, faculty, and administration, modeled after our national legislative and executive branch. Even though the student body numbered more than 750, the student council managed the open meetings quite well. Over the three years that I witnessed these meetings, the students were able to respectfully debate a number of controversial bills.

In short, schools can do much to improve practice in the area of student governance. The road to success must include giving students important decision-making power, establishing solid membership criteria, and developing a sound plan for a truly inclusive governing body.

Students on Committees

A common approach to involving students in school affairs is to have them sit on committees. Despite its broad application and frequent use, this can be one of the least effective ways to honor student ideas. Adding a student or two on a committee of teachers or other adults can easily take on an aura of tokenism. I have sat on many a committee with a few student members, and I've seen the students become frustrated as well-meaning adults asked them to weigh in on a matter, only to have the committee totally ignore their comments. If we ask, we must also be willing to listen! If we want to develop citizenship skills, we cannot treat students like second-class citizens.

All committee work runs into the push and pull of minority and majority opinion; that is part of the group process. However, we must take special care when we bring students into the mix. Nothing derails student voice faster than inviting students to go out on a limb to express their views—and then dismissing those views. It's demoralizing for a student leadership group to spend months hammering out a new dress code policy, only to have the school board reject the proposal. School leaders who set out to enhance student voice would do much better to start with student involvement in projects they are relatively sure they can support. Once the students cut their teeth, gain some credibility, and understand the possibility of setbacks, addressing the student dress code might be a reasonable choice.

Whenever possible, student membership on a committee should approach parity with other committee members. A ten-member committee might have three students, three parents, and three teachers along with a committee chair. I never place a lone student on a committee; if student representation needs to be minimal, I send two students.

The most important determinant for student membership is the purpose or mission of the committee. When we created committees as part of our accreditation process, we asked two students to serve on each committee. The standards of accreditation require student membership on committees, but the committees are not decision-making bodies, so the numbers don't matter as much. Students are there to provide student viewpoints, and two student members accomplish this objective nicely. At times it is appropriate to have a committee made up entirely of students. For example, a student committee might be charged with making recommendations to school administration about proposed improvements in the school's advisory program, while parallel committees of parents and teachers address the same topic.

Years ago, I stumbled upon a wonderful process that helped our high school revamp a tired, ineffective procedure for reporting student progress midway through each marking period. I had thirty teachers spend several hours brainstorming what they thought should happen; at the same time, thirty students tackled the same issue in another room, and thirty parents in a third. We then brought the three groups together in six cross-site meeting groups to share the ideas generated. As you might imagine, the different groups had specific and sometimes conflicting ideas about how progress reports needed to be done—but at least now the differences were out in the open. The activity ended with the faculty developing a new protocol for progress reports that better accommodated the expressed needs of students and parents.

This exercise illustrates an attempt to balance voices in committee work. When we ask people to give of their time and ideas, we need to make a commitment to consider and value their work.

Student Interviewers

One arena where student voice can have a powerful effect is the committee that screens and interviews job candidates. Given the strict hiring guidelines of today's litigious world, it may be difficult to envision involving students in the hiring process. Yet this too can have a significantly positive impact on students and school programs. Student participation in the screening and interviewing process accomplishes some important objectives. First, it sends a clear signal to applicants about the role of students in this school. Whenever I experienced student involvement in jobs that I was applying for, my enthusiasm for the position soared. I knew this was a school that aimed to be student-centered.

I owe my first high school principalship, in part, to a student I'll call Joe, a member of the interviewing committee at Leavitt Area High School. Joe had gone on a site visit at Orono High School, where I had served as assistant principal for seven years until taking a position as a middle school principal in another district two years before the visit. It was a bit awkward to have a committee visit a school where I no longer worked, but they wanted to research my high school experiences. The story goes that Joe walked into the Orono High School cafeteria during lunch and made a beeline for the rowdiest table in the room. He sat down and introduced himself to a handful of the school's least compliant seniors, telling them he was there to get the low-down on a guy named Beaudoin. The Orono students had little trouble remembering me; they had been frequent visitors to my office as ninth and tenth graders. I never found out exactly what they said, but Joe became a strong supporter of my candidacy after talking with these students. As I think back on this event, I suspect that I can attribute my professional path to Joe's bold move—and to a double dose of student voice in action.

Another important benefit of involving students in the hiring process is that it boosts support from the student body for the resulting new hires. Joe and other student committee members must have spoken positively to friends about the incoming principal. I felt a little more like the students' choice as I entered my new position.

The key to involving students in the hiring process is to have a clearly defined protocol. Students can and should be trusted to adhere to the rules involving confidentiality and anonymity. In most districts, the protocols for interviewing committees are fairly clear and have been reviewed by legal counsel. It should be a reasonably straightforward matter to check these against the reality of student participation.

Student Representation on the School Board

I have worked in two districts that allow school leaders to appoint student representatives to the school board. Though the practice is not common, my experiences with it have been very positive. Students take their responsibility quite seriously, and board members appreciate their input. The program creates a win-win situation: The student body looks at how the board works, and board members are reminded of the student perspective that their deliberations should honor. Adults see what young people can do, and students gain appreciation for the adults' dedication. What a great introduction to the responsibilities of citizenship!

Maine state statutes allow only elected board members to vote. However, the chairperson of the Kennebunk School Board introduced a straw vote protocol: Students are allowed to indicate yea or nay on a topic, even though their "vote" is not actually counted. This gives them more input and allows the public at the meeting or those watching the TV broadcast to know their stance.

Included below is the draft proposal for the program at School Administrative District 71 in Kennebunk, Maine. Adopted in August of 2004, this is evolving into an important component of student voice in our district.

Student Board Members

Purpose

The Board believes it is important to seek out and consider students' ideas, viewpoints and reactions to the educational program. In order to provide student input and involvement, the Board shall appoint two student Board members selected in accordance with procedures established at Kennebunk High School and approved by the Board.

Participation

Two student Board members shall be seated with regular Board members and be recognized at meetings as advisory, nonvoting members. They may fully participate in meetings by questioning presenters and discussing issues. Student Board members will receive all materials presented to Board members except those related to closed sessions or confidential in nature.

Term

The term of a student Board member shall be from July 1st of one year to June 30th of the following year. The Board shall act on appointments for the next term at the June meeting or at the earliest possible subsequent meeting. Should a vacancy occur prior to the conclusion of the term, another student may be appointed in accordance with established procedures to complete the term.

Eligibility

Student Board members shall maintain curriculum and citizenship standards which include:

A cumulative 3.0 G.P.A. (Grade Point Average).

Standards of behavior and citizenship that are determined to be of high quality.

Adherence to standards of membership, attendance, and decorum.

A student Board member may be removed from office by a ⅔ vote of the Board for cause.

Elective Credit

Students appointed as student Board members may be awarded one elective credit (½ credit for Semester I and ½ credit for Semester II) for participation under the provisions of an independent study contract, subject to prior approval of the principal. Credit will be awarded based on a written self-reflection and verification of attendance and participation by the Board chair at the conclusion of each semester.

Reimbursement of Expenses

Student Board members may be reimbursed for expenses incurred in meeting responsibilities of the position, but shall not receive compensation for attendance at Board meetings to which regular Board members may be entitled.

Kennebunk High School
Student Board Members
Selection Procedures

Note: These procedures are temporary. They are intended to provide the School Board with recommendations for Student Board members for the 2004–2005 school year. This procedure will be reviewed and adjusted prior to June 2005 as part of the school's First Amendment Grant action plan, which calls for the development of a comprehensive governance procedure at K.H.S. All Juniors (Class of 2005) will be notified of the need for two student Board members and all eligible will be encouraged to make application.

Eligibility

Applicants must have a 3.0 G.P.A. (Grade Point Average) and a record of high quality behavior and citizenship. Applicants will be asked to write a brief essay expressing their reasons for applying and the contribution they hope to make.

The Principal and the Leadership Team will review applications. If needed, the faculty and student counsel will be involved in screening candidates.

Recommendations will be brought to the Board for approval, hopefully, in June.

Recommend that students take part in an orientation prior to attending a meeting.

This could be with the full Board or a sub committee of the Board.

Recommend that the role of student Board members be part of the full Board orientation.

Addition of two students will create some challenges.

More time at meetings (two more voices).

Logistics of the meeting space.

Attention to confidentiality issues by both Central Office and Board members (including obvious issues involving contract negotiations, personnel matters, and individual student disciplinary information.)

Students will take this seriously, so expect challenges and ideas from them. They will expect that equal weight will be given to their opinions.

It might be necessary to provide some informal interaction between students and Board chair to help them navigate the meeting process.

Draft—Student Board Member Application
for the Class of 2005

Name:

Please answer the following questions:

1. Do you have a 3.0 GPA or higher?

2. Can you commit to attending school board meetings every first and second Monday of the month, typically 7:00 p.m. to 10:00 p.m.?

3. List any school and/or out-of-school activities that you are involved in, to show that you have high quality behavior and citizenship skills.

4. Write a brief essay expressing your reason for applying and the contribution you hope to make.

Please return to Mr. Beaudoin by Monday, June 7th at 2:30 p.m.

Levels of Responsibility

To educate our students to become contributing citizens in our schools and beyond, we must make an effort to clearly define expectations. My wife, Sharon, found a simple rubric to explain to students the levels of responsibility needed to contribute in a positive way to our school climate. I've used this strategy for more than fifteen years to help students understand their roles as citizens of the school. Meeting with student groups on the first day of the school year, I outline a basic four-point rubric for levels of responsibility:

1. Not meeting the standard

2. Partially meeting the standard

3. Meeting the standard

4. Exceeding the standard

Even with high school students, I use a paper towel as a prop to explain expectations for these levels of responsibility. A person at level one might do something awful with the paper towel, such as plugging a toilet so that others could not use it or the custodian had to do extra work to restore it to service. A person at level two might not cause actual damage with the paper towel but would carelessly miss the trash can when discarding it, then leave it for someone else to pick up. The person who met the standard would use the paper towel properly, and then place it in the trashcan, scoring a three. The people who exceeded expectations to reach level four would not only properly take care of their own paper towels, but even bend over and pick up a towel someone else had dropped. Weeks after this introduction to civic responsibility, I hear students bragging about being a level 4 when they do something for the greater good.

This simple rubric can be used to teach and promote standards in all aspects of conduct. Several years ago, my current school district established a code of conduct, part of which is shown here. All of the core values and the behavioral expectations surrounding them can be broken down in a four-point rubric. What a wonderful school we would have if all students and adults would achieve a level three in each of these areas!

Maine School Administrative District 71
Code of Conduct

MSAD 71 is committed to maintaining a supportive and orderly school environment in which students may receive and staff may deliver a quality education without disruption or interference. This environment ensures that students will develop as ethical, responsible and involved citizens.

To achieve this goal, MSAD 71 has established a set of expectations for conduct. These expectations are based on the values identified by the school community as essential to ethical and responsible behavior.

Core Values

Respect: treating themselves, others and the environment with consideration

Honesty: acting truthfully in all academic endeavors and interpersonal relationships

Compassion: responding with care and concern when dealing with the limitations and sufferings of others

Fairness: showing integrity in all dealings with others

Responsibility: being accountable for personal actions, both as an individual and as a member of the community

Courage: behaving with conviction in the face of personal or ethical challenges

Maine School Administrative District 71 has high standards for ethical and responsible behavior and holds individuals within our organization accountable for their actions. The following expectations are set to guide behavior, attitudes and interactions.

Expectations for Behavior

Students and adults in our district are expected to be:

Respectful	Help maintain an atmosphere of respect, dignity and trust
Kind	Demonstrate an open-minded attitude, fairness, and tolerance
Collaborative	Utilize conflict resolution skills and creative problem solving
Sincere	Practice honesty, integrity, perseverance and good sportsmanship
Unselfish	Participate in service to the school and larger community
Environmentally Aware	Assume responsibility regarding environmental issues
Accountable	Take responsibility for actions and recognize the rights of others
Involved	Be an informed and concerned citizen, aware of the rights and obligations within a democratic society

The Code applies to students and adults who are on school property, who are in attendance at school or at any school-sponsored activity, or whose conduct at any time or place directly interferes with the operations, discipline, or general welfare of the school.

The board recognizes the need to define unacceptable student conduct, identify the possible consequences for unacceptable conduct, and ensure that discipline is administered fairly, promptly, and appropriately.

If we can do a good job of defining expectations and supporting students as they strive to meet our standards, we are really preparing them for citizenship. We are preparing young people to contribute to society in positive ways by assuming responsibility.

A Mission-Driven School

The following mission statement drives decision-making at Kennebunk High School.

Mission Statement

Kennebunk High School is committed to providing a varied and rigorous academic program. Within a safe and caring environment, each student will be encouraged to realize his/her fullest potential and become a lifelong learner, as well as a responsible member of society.

Academic Expectations:

Students at Kennebunk High School will demonstrate mastery of these academic skills in each of the required content areas.

- Reading
- Communication
- Problem solving
- Use of technology
- Research

Social and Civic Expectations:

Students at Kennebunk High School are expected to

- Demonstrate a spirit of cooperation and teamwork.
- Help maintain an atmosphere of respect, dignity and trust.
- Demonstrate an open-minded attitude, fairness and tolerance.
- Practice honesty, integrity, perseverance and good sportsmanship.
- Take responsibility for actions and recognize the rights of others.
- Participate in service to the school and larger community.
- Be informed and concerned citizens, aware of their rights and obligations within a democratic society.
- Value creative expression.

It is not difficult to see how this mission statement could be used at our school to promote student voice, participation, citizenship and leadership. The social and civic expectations echo many of the core values found in the MSAD 71 Code of Conduct. The mission statement helps everyone in our organization focus on what is most important. The fact that the approved mission statement is so simple and straightforward makes success more certain. Any school trying to increase student responsibility would be well advised to write a mission statement that advances the civic behaviors it desires.

7

Highlighting the First Amendment

Congress shall make no law respecting an establishment of religion, or prohibiting the free exercise thereof; or abridging the freedom of speech, or of the press; or the right of the people peaceably to assemble, and to petition the Government for a redress of grievances.

— First Amendment to the U.S. Constitution

A Second-Rate Issue?

A recent Associated Press article by Ben Feller[17] highlights our schools' deficiencies in educating for citizenship. The article's headline reads, "Freedom of what? First Amendment no big deal, students say." Much of what Feller wrote deserves scrutiny as we look at the idea of educating for citizenship.

Feller begins by saying that the First Amendment is a second-rate issue among young people; many of them do not understand what is protected by the bedrock of the Bill of Rights. The article was based on a survey[18] conducted by researchers at the University of Connecticut among more than 100,000 students, 8,000 teachers and 500 administrators from 544 public and private high schools. Feller writes, "The study suggests that

---

17 Biddeford (Maine) Journal Tribune, January 31, 2005.
18 Knight Foundation, AP, 2004.

students will only embrace First Amendment freedoms if they are taught about them and are given an opportunity to practice them, but schools don't make the matter a priority." Students not only show little understanding of their protected freedoms, they also show little passion for them.

Feller quotes Hodding Carter III, president of the John S. and James L. Knight Foundation, which funded the study: "These results are not only disturbing; they are dangerous. Ignorance about the basics of our free society is a danger to our nation's future." Feller goes on to discuss the lack of opportunity for students in our high schools to practice their basic freedoms.

Nearly three-quarters of the high school students responding to the University of Connecticut survey said they didn't know how they felt about the First Amendment, or took it for granted. When asked if people should be allowed to express unpopular opinions, 83% of the students agreed, compared to a 97% affirmative response from teachers and 99% from principals. Only 51% of the students felt that newspapers should be allowed to publish freely without government approval of stories. Yet 70% of them felt that musicians should be allowed to sing songs with offensive lyrics. This was one area where our youth were more intense than adults, as just 58% of the teachers and 43% of principals supported such leniency. More than half of the students also felt that they should be allowed to report controversial issues in their school newspaper without the approval of school authorities. These results show just how far our students are from grasping the basic freedoms they have and how these apply to schools.

Educating for Freedom and Responsibility

Fortunately, not all the news is bad. School leaders who want to teach citizenship do have somewhere to turn. For Kennebunk High School, the opportunity came in the form of an invitation to join the First Amendment Schools (FAS) network, co-sponsored by the Association for Supervision and Curriculum Development (ASCD) and the First Amendment Center.

First Amendment Schools: Educating for Freedom and Responsibility is "a national reform initiative designed to transform how schools practice and teach the rights and responsibilities that frame civic life in our democracy."[19] According to its Web site, the project has four primary goals:

♦ Create consensus guidelines and guiding principles for all schools interested in creating and sustaining First Amendment principles in their school;

♦ Establish Project Schools, in every region of the nation, where First Amendment principles are understood and applied throughout the school community;

♦ Encourage and develop curriculum reforms that reinvigorate and deepen teaching about the First Amendment across the curriculum; and

♦ Educate school leaders, teachers, school board members and attorneys, and other key stakeholders about the meaning and significance of First Amendment principles and ideals.

In the spring of 2004, several educational consultants encouraged Kennebunk High School to apply for membership as a Project School. Upon receiving the grant application, I reviewed it with a student leader. It didn't seem to fit our needs—in fact, its very power and formality seemed a bit threatening to the fairly comfortable plateau we had reached in student voice initiatives—so we tossed it out. However, the idea resurfaced several weeks later at a school reform conference. Once we learned more about the FAS network, we changed our minds. Eight students and I formed a team to prepare the application.

The grant writing process was a fantastic learning opportunity for all involved. We discovered that our school very much followed the principles set forth by the First Amendment Schools initiative, even though we did so instinctively rather than by conscious design. I was impressed with the passion and wisdom that our students brought to this effort. Nevertheless, we sent off the completed grant proposal with little real hope of

---

[19] www.firstamendmentschools.org, accessed July 28, 2005.

being one of five schools nationwide selected to join the net-work, launched with ten schools just two years before.

A month or so later, we received word that our school had been awarded the grant! Soon we were off to a FAS conference in Washington, D.C, where our five-member committee joined fourteen other groups for a process of sharing, planning, and learning. Since then, we have found so many pluses for our school: a network of like-minded schools, wonderful resources from the grant sponsors, and a framework for school improve-ment imbedded in democratic principles. We were amazed at how far our student voice initiative had brought us.

The following information from the First Amendment Schools initiative summarizes the purpose of this program and offers a glimpse of its richness.

First Amendment Schools: Vision Statement

The Challenge

First Amendment Schools are built on the conviction that the five freedoms protected by the first amendment are a cornerstone of American democracy and essential for citizenship in a diverse society.

For more than 200 years, the First Amendment has been at the heart of history's boldest and most successful experiment in lib-erty. We readily acknowledge that the United States failed to live up to its founding principles in 1791, and that the nation still has a distance to go in the 21st century. But the history of our nation is the story of the ongoing struggle to extend the promise of free-dom more fully and fairly to each and every citizen.

Today the need to sustain and expand our experiment in liberty is made more urgent by the challenge of living with our deepest differences in a diverse and complex society. The need to commit ourselves as a people to the rights and responsibilities that flow from the First Amendment has never been more vital—or more difficult. At a time in our history when we most need to reaffirm what we share as citizens across our differences, the ignorance and contention now surrounding the First Amendment threaten to divide the nation and undermine our freedom.

The key place to address this challenge is in our schools, the institutions most responsible for transmitting civic principles and virtues to each succeeding generation.

Schools must not only teach the First Amendment; they must also find ways to model and apply the democratic first principles that they are charged with teaching. The rights and responsibilities of the First Amendment provide a much-needed civic framework for reaffirming and renewing the civic aims of education.

Guiding Principles

We envision First Amendment Schools as places where all members of the school community practice the civic habits of the heart necessary to sustain a free people that would remain free. Schools may carry out this mission in ways that vary greatly, depending on the age of the students, the size of the school, the needs of the local community and whether the school is public or private. What unites First Amendment Schools is not one view of democratic education or the First Amendment, but rather an abiding commitment to teach and model the rights and responsibilities that undergird the First Amendment.

We propose the following four principles as foundational for creating and sustaining a First Amendment School:

I. Create Laboratories of Democratic Freedom

The future of the American Republic depends upon instilling in young citizens an abiding commitment to the democratic first principles that sustain our experiment in liberty.

First Amendment Schools educate for freedom by providing students and all members of the school community with substantial opportunities to practice democracy. Knowledge of our framing documents and the structure and functions of government is important, but preparation for citizenship also requires virtues and skills acquired through participation in decision-making. By practicing democracy, students confront the challenges of

(cont'd.)

self-government, including the difficult task of balancing a commitment to individual rights with a concern for the common good.

First Amendment Schools create organizational structures, allocate time and resources, and develop policies and curricula designed to support and promote democratic learning communities. Pedagogical decisions, including instructional and assessment practices, extend opportunities for authentic learning that inform a citizen's understanding of the world beyond the classroom.

First Amendment Schools include administrators, teachers, staff, students, parents and community members when making decisions about organization, governance and curricula. When everyone is given a meaningful voice in shaping the life of the school, all have a real stake in creating and sustaining safe and caring learning communities. All members of the school community should have opportunities to exercise leadership, negotiate differences, propose solutions to shared problems and practice other skills essential to thoughtful and effective participation in civic life.

II. Commit to Inalienable Rights and Civic Responsibility

Freedom of religions, speech, press, assembly and petition are fundamental and inalienable rights. All Americans have a civic responsibility to guard these rights for every citizen.

First Amendment Schools are dedicated to educating for citizenship by teaching and modeling the democratic principles of the Constitution of the United States. Schools take this mission seriously by providing all members of the school community with daily opportunities to exercise their constitutional rights with responsibility.

First Amendment Schools uphold the principles of freedom and democracy when they protect religious liberty rights, encourage freedom of expression, promote academic freedom, ensure a free student press and support broad-based involvement in school governance. Acting responsibly, students, teachers, administrators, staff, parents and community members can do much to uphold the rights of every citizen.

III. Include All Stakeholders

The First Amendment provides the civic framework of rights and responsibilities that enables Americans to work together for the common good in schools and communities.

First Amendment Schools affirm the importance of modeling the democratic process and upholding individual rights in the development of policies and curricula. Decisions are made after appropriate involvement of those affected by the decision and with due consideration for the rights of those holding dissenting views.

First Amendment Schools recognize that parents have the primary responsibility for the upbringing and education of their children. All Americans, however, share an important stake in educating students for responsible citizenship in a free society. Students and schools benefit greatly when parents, students, educators and community members work closely together to promote a shared vision of the First Amendment throughout the school culture and across the community.

IV. Translate Civic Education into Community Engagement

A society committed to freedom and justice for all requires citizens with the knowledge, virtues and skills needed for active engagement in public life.

First Amendment Schools encourage active citizenship by giving students opportunities to translate civic education into community engagement. Active citizens are willing to participate in public life by addressing problems and issues in their communities, our nation and the world.

First Amendment Schools provide opportunities for students to learn civic virtue and moral character throughout the school culture and across the curriculum. Students are encouraged to demonstrate an active concern for the welfare of others through service learning and civic problem-solving. First Amendment rights are best guarded and civic responsibilities best exercised when citizens are actively engaged in building a more just and free society.

(cont'd.)

A Shared Vision

These guiding principles are offered as a shared vision for schools seeking to fulfill the promise of freedom under the First Amendment.

Learning about freedom and justice, however important, can never be enough; educating for democratic citizenship must be more than an academic exercise. If we are to sustain and expand the American experiment in liberty, young citizens must acquire the civic skills and virtues needed to exercise their freedom with responsibility.

We invite all schools and every citizen to join us in affirming these principles and putting them into action. The time has come for all Americans to work together to renew our shared commitment to the civic principles and virtues vital to democracy, freedom and the common good.

www.firstamendmentschools.org

Core Civic Habits Practiced in First Amendment Schools

All members of a First Amendment School community understand that the five freedoms of the First Amendment provide a civic framework within which we are able to debate our differences, understand one another, and serve the common good. All students who graduate from these schools, K–12, embody this understanding by demonstrating the civic habits of heart, mind, voice, and work.

Civic Habits of Work

+ Connect convictions and actions with integrity and moral purpose
+ Work with integrity and persistence toward the common good
+ Integrate passions and deepest values into work
+ Work to counter prejudice and discrimination
+ Demonstrate self-discipline

Civic Habits of Mind

♦ Value inquiry that encourages and appreciates both complexity and ambiguity

♦ Demonstrate knowledge of democratic principles, human rights, and social justice

♦ Practice critical reflection of self and others

♦ Understand how to participate in the political process and democratic institutions that shape public policy

Civic Habits of Voice

♦ Listen and observe deeply, and respond in a connected way

♦ Strive to exercise free speech responsibly

♦ Speak out on matters of conscience

♦ Agree and disagree honestly and respectfully

♦ Believe that how we debate, not only what we debate is critical

Civic Habits of Heart

♦ Take responsibility for self and others

♦ Demonstrate clarity of moral purpose

♦ Show concern for the welfare of others

♦ Act with courage and compassion

♦ Practice forgiveness and humility

♦ Resolve differences in constructive ways

All Members of the School Community

♦ See the four civic habits as a foundation for exercising freedom with responsibility

♦ Exercise leadership for social justice

♦ Understand, promote and model First Amendment principles in their lives

♦ Balance individual interest with the common good

♦ Protect the rights of others, especially those with whom they disagree

♦ Encourage the inclusion of multiple perspectives in the public square

(cont'd.)

> ◆ Value and demonstrate honesty and personal integrity
> ◆ Understand and consider the long term consequences of their actions
>
> Practicing the four basic civic habits is a shared responsibility among school, home and community, and results in citizens actively engaged in public life and working toward the common good.
>
> *www.firstamendmentschools.org*

At the end of our first year as a First Amendment School, we are just scratching the surface of ways that we can create a more democratic school. In a year-end evaluation, our students felt that as a school we had a great deal of student voice, but that our work needed growth in three important areas. Students expressed concern about the lack of cohesion among all the voice initiatives and stressed a need for better communication and clarity. They also saw our involvement of young people as somewhat exclusionary—there were still kids on the outside wishing they could become involved and wondering how to join the fun. Finally, our students concluded that although our school currently had a great attitude about empowering students, we still needed to flesh out a formalized governance structure that would protect these opportunities over time.

And so, our journey continues.

8

Finding Inspiration for the Journey

Educators and school leaders who set out to promote student voice need not find their own way, and they do not travel this road alone. Other schools offer models of educational practice, school governance, and community involvement that can guide their efforts. Remarkable individuals stand as beacons to light the way. Finally, networks of schools pursuing similar goals offer companionship, encouragement, leadership, and resources for the journey. This chapter highlights just a few of the schools, individuals, and networks that have inspired and supported my own efforts over the years.

Barnstable: Service Learning on Cape Cod

We have already noted the value of service learning as a teaching strategy that can positively impact youth learning. Students who plan their own learning within an academic context find the process empowering, but more importantly, they experience apprentice citizenship. The following pages summarize the work of one school system in the quest to graduate civic-minded young men and women.

The town of Barnstable, Massachusetts, provides an excellent model for civic engagement among youth. Located on Cape

Cod, south of Boston, Barnstable has experienced some challenging demographic shifts over the past few decades. The traditionally strong tourist industry continues to dominate the economic landscape, but more and more retirees and older professionals are moving into the area. As a result, rising property values have made it increasingly unlikely that young adults can afford to settle in the community where they grew up. Funding for schools becomes increasingly difficult as the tax base shifts away from the school-age population.

The high school has an enrollment of approximately 2000 students; about 1000 students attend the middle school. The faculty and administration at the two schools have taken some interesting steps to address the challenges facing the community. One of the most notable accomplishments has been the reconfiguration of a Youth Commission that informs the work of the town council. Once made up of eight adults and four students, the commission now comprises five students between the ages of 13 and 18, elected by their peers, along with two nonvoting adults. In an effort to be more inclusive, the community also has formed a larger advisory committee, made up of any adult or student who wishes to participate, that makes recommendations to the youth council.

Janice Barton, elected to the Barnstable Town Council in 2003, is a member of the council's School Committee subcommittee and also serves as the council's liaison to the Youth Commission. She pushed hard for the ordinance that changed its configuration. Passed in November 2004, the ordinance also added youth services to the community service strand on the town organizational flow chart for the first time. Barton hopes that student voices will generate more youth advocacy among governmental decision makers, and she doesn't hesitate to bring youth issues to the town council's attention at every meeting. As she often reminds her colleagues, "Children are our most valuable and vulnerable natural resource." This work to strengthen youth voice on the town council illustrates how community agencies can partner with students to address important community needs and problems.

A strong advocate for service learning as a vehicle to empower youth, Barton is one of many officials in Barnstable who promote this teaching strategy to address both student and community needs. A strong service learning program is emerging in the Barnstable school system. Among the many rich service learning activities was an exit poll conducted on election day in November 2004 by high school psychology classes taught by Sophia Sarhanis and Janet Mohre. Gathering data from 1,427 voters spanning 13 different precincts, the students analyzed the results and compiled a 75-page report[20] of their findings. The exit polls asked respondents to identify themselves by age, gender, party affiliation, and precinct, and then asked about the significance of various issues. As an example of the students' findings, the report stated that all age brackets ranked the issues in essentially the same order of significance: The war on terror led the list, followed by health care, education, and international relations, with the environment in last place. The only major exception to this trend was that the 18–22 and 31–45 age groups found education more important than health care. This rigorous experience helped the high school students to better understand the election process, interact with the voting public, and inform town officials of their findings. In short, this work helped these young people become more connected to their community's civic responsibilities.

At a recent KIDS[21] Consortium conference on connecting the classroom and community, I met a woman whose job title is one of the longest I've ever encountered: Communities and Schools for Success (CS2) Entrepreneur with the Center for Youth Development and Education: Commonwealth Corporation in Boston. In her work with the Barnstable Public Schools, Bobbi Moritz has tirelessly promoted service learning. In our brief conversation, she cited a number of ways that the Barnstable service learning program is working to connect students with the issues of their day. The examples of intergenerational, environmental, civic and humanitarian focuses for the students' learning

---

[20] www.barnstable.k12.ma.us/bhs/SocStud/Sar_Mohre/index.htm, accessed July 28, 2005.
[21] KIDS Consortium (215 Lisbon Street, Lewiston, Maine 04240 and www.kids-consortium.org).

left me convinced that the students of Barnstable are on their way to becoming active citizens.

Mark Grashow: A Mosquito in Brooklyn

Anita Roddick, founder of The Body Shop, has been quoted as saying, "If you think you are too small and insignificant to make a difference, you've never slept with a mosquito in the room." Whenever I hear that statement or one of its many variations, I think of a retired New York City schoolteacher named Mark Grashow.

Grashow and I met in the spring of 2002 at a conference in Providence, Rhode Island, sponsored by the Brown Educational Alliance. We had shared the stage for one of the sessions. Along with five students, I spoke about student voice; Grashow spoke of the importance of knowing students well. The gist of his message was that we can't educate students effectively unless we know their circumstances—how often they ate a meal with their parents, how much sleep they got each night, or whether they worked outside of school. Grashow had developed a survey to gather this information. The cumulative results he presented showed the tough challenges facing many of today's youth—but what I found most impressive was how deeply Mark Grashow cared, and what he had done about it.

As a longtime advisor for the Key Club at Abraham Lincoln High School in Brooklyn, Grashow had made student exchange trips the centerpiece of this group's activities. Following our presentations, as we sat down for lunch, Grashow complimented my students on their presentation and suggested that we consider an exchange. The students were enthusiastic, Grashow was persistent, and before I knew it, 35 Brooklyn students from Lincoln, Dewey High School, and Brooklyn Tech arrived for three October days in Kennebunk, Maine—a place they affectionately dubbed "Pleasantville." Their group seemed to include students from all over the world. Lincoln High School's population is 35 percent foreign born, with large numbers from the former Soviet Union, India, Pakistan, South America, Mexico, Asia and the Caribbean. The remaining 65 percent of the students are almost equally divided among Caucasian, Hispanic, and Black.

In March, my students reciprocated by spending three days in the Big Apple. By any measure, the experience was fantastic. The itinerary included visits to Ellis Island, Ground Zero, the Metropolitan Museum of Art, and Broadway. Students from both communities got a wonderful view of another part of the world. They learned about people from totally different ethnic backgrounds and cultures, but more importantly, developed strong bonds of friendship. I knew we had struck gold when I saw my students sprinting alongside the New Yorkers' bus as it headed home. To this day, Kennebunk High School students find the exchange a highlight of their senior year.

To me, Mark Grashow represents all those people in America's schools who teach to make a difference for kids—people who put kids first. A teacher for 33 years, Grashow was twice honored as high school teacher of the year for the Brooklyn and Staten Island schools. He also coached, chaired the school's teachers union chapter, and served on numerous boards and committees, but I believe his legacy lies in the hundreds upon hundreds of students he touched through his work with the Key Club.

The Key Club is a service organization whose members make contributions, large and small, to their school and community. Students are involved in some 30 activities each year, ranging from an open house at Halloween (complete with a haunted basement) for a thousand neighborhood youngsters, to street fairs, to holiday parties at a shelter for battered women. In return, the students gain a feeling of accomplishment, a sense of belonging that plays a huge role in their development.

When Kennebunk High School participated in its first exchange four years ago, Mark Grashow had already retired from teaching. Yet he still organizes several major exchanges annually, involving a number of neighboring high schools. He has organized and hosted regional exchanges with Key Clubs from the New York towns of Ogdensburg, Canandaigua, Watertown, Latham, East Aurora, and Sparta. Over the years, through international exchanges with communities as far afield as Holbaek,

Denmark; Majorca, Spain; Nagano, Japan; Venice, Italy; Vienna, Austria; and Avellino, Italy, he has touched the lives of students all over the world.

He sets high standards for his students—a must for embarking with them on exchanges in the United States and abroad—and they deliver. They take on much of the work involved in organizing the exchanges. In my view, Mark Grashow is a perfect example of the educator who provides students with the protective factors that Bonnie Benard[22] cites in her research on student resiliency: caring relationships, high expectations, and opportunities to participate and contribute.

If all this isn't enough, Grashow has been extensively involved in a program to support schools in Africa during the past several years. He describes the Africa Project as "amazing." He has helped organize the United States–Africa Children's Fellowship, which pairs up thirteen New York schools with thirteen schools in Bulawayo, Zimbabwe. He and his wife, Sheri, visited Africa in July 2005 to see their first container of donated materials delivered to Zimbabwe—more than 20,000 books as well as an incredible amount of school supplies. The organization hopes to expand to 35 schools in the 2005-2006 school year.

There is still a lot of sting in this Brooklyn mosquito.

Federal Hocking High School:
A Laboratory of Democracy

Federal Hocking High School serves 400 students in grades 9—12 in Stewart, Ohio. For more than a decade, the school community, under the leadership of principal Dr. George Wood, has been working to become a more democratic institution. Federal Hocking is an inaugural member and leading representative of the First Amendment Schools project. In fact, it was Dr. Wood and several former Federal Hocking students who convinced me that Kennebunk High School should seek to join the network; far from being restrictive, they said, participation would

---

[22] Bonnie Benard, *Resiliency:What We Have Learned*, 2004.

support our work in the areas of student voice and educating for democracy.

The gains achieved at Federal Hocking reflect its community's support for the idea that the purpose of education is to serve—in Wood's words—as "democracy's finishing school, the last shared experience for citizens in our republic and the place where we can inculcate the virtues of civic life."[23] Everything from classroom teaching practices to school governance to the organization of the school day centers on developing a democratic community.

Teachers have responsibility for major decisions regarding the curriculum. Socratic seminars enrich classroom experiences with a student-centered approach. Students have a strong voice in school decisions, with representation on the school board, in hiring committees, and in many other school organizations. They have worked to clarify the school dress code and revise the student handbook; they run the Senior Project Night and the Intersession program. Given greater freedom, students at Federal Hocking took on greater responsibility, and they have flourished in this setting: The school has seen higher test scores, a higher graduation rate, a greater number of students going on to college, and fewer disciplinary referrals.

The fact that Federal Hocking High School was selected as a First Amendment Schools project school has only served to bolster their work on becoming a laboratory of democracy. According to Wood, "Becoming a First Amendment School has allowed our community to review its efforts, examine additional ways to engage the school community, and push forward on our work to insure that democracy is not just a slogan, but a way of life."

Quest High School: A Texas Dynamo

I first met the folks from Quest High School at a two-day service learning conference in Washington D.C. during the summer of 2000. Among the presenters was Kim Huseman, the service

---

[23] See www.firstamendmentschools.org/involve/federalhockinghigh.html, accessed July 28, 2005.

learning coordinator at Quest High School in Humble, Texas. My students and I sat in on several discussion groups with Huseman and were impressed with her program and her passion for her work. Quest High School sounded like a very dynamic school.

Fast-forward three months to the Coalition of Essential Schools (CES) Fall Forum in Providence, Rhode Island. There, I attended sessions presented by Kim Huseman and Cecilia Hawkins, then the school's principal, featuring their advisory program and service learning program. Again, I found the sessions both informative and inspiring.

Over the next five years, it seemed that my students and I bumped into Quest High School representatives at conference after conference. Like Kennebunk High School, Quest never missed an opportunity to attend the CES Fall Forums. As National Service Learning Leader Schools, we each sent contingents to the annual National Service Learning Conferences. I was not surprised to see Quest High School named a First Amendment Schools project school, and we met up again in Washington, D.C., to take advantage of the rich resources of that new affiliation. The more I learned about Quest and its programs, the more I appreciated the opportunity to connect and reconnect with its educators—and for my students to connect and reconnect with its students. I could not ask for a better example of the camaraderie, support, guidance, and inspiration that school leaders can draw from networks of schools pursuing similar goals.

Quest opened its doors in 1995 as a magnet school, one of three high schools in the Humble Independent School District. Current enrollment is approximately 240 students in grades 9–12. The school was created based on the following beliefs:[24]

♦ All students can learn given the right conditions and motivations.

♦ Students should be at the center of the learning process.

♦ Students learn more effectively when the material is relevant and interesting to them.

---

[24] See www.qhs.humble.k12.tx.us, accessed July 28, 2005.

♦ Learning is on-going throughout life.

♦ The learning process must be collaborative and interactive.

♦ Students are responsible for their own learning; teachers are responsible for facilitating learning.

♦ The school should provide a safe and nurturing environment for learning.

♦ The school should prepare students to function in the world as effective and competent participants in the community.

♦ There should be an active partnership among parents, community and the school.

♦ Education is a foundation of our society and impacts both the immediate quality of our lives and the future of civilization.

♦ Small schools improve a student's education by ensuring educators truly know and understand a student's needs and learning styles.

♦ Students learn by doing.

♦ Students must learn how to learn.

Building on these strong foundational beliefs, the high school has garnered (in less than a decade) an impressive list of affiliations and grant support. Quest belongs to the Coalition of Essential Schools and has been designated one of the Coalition's 20 Mentor High Schools because of its commitment to a small school configuration. Quest is also one of two schools in Texas recognized as a Beacon School by the Annenberg Foundation, which awarded Quest an Annenberg Challenge Grant in 1997. In 2002, the Character Education Partnership named the school a National School of Character. This followed the 2001 distinction honoring the high school as a National Service Learning Leader School. Selected as a First Amendment Schools project school in the spring of 2004, Quest has also received substantial funding from the Telecommunications Infrastructure Fund Board to support updated technology and expand student access and use of the Internet.

Dr. Lawrence Kohn succeeded Cecilia Hawkins as principal at Quest High School after she became the district's assistant superintendent. The school's First Amendment School profile describes Quest as founded on the principles of shared leadership and decision-making. "These principles," explains Kohn, "include not only staff members but students, parents, and community members as well." Student voice has been critical in making decisions about policy, curriculum and operational practices during the school's first decade. "Yet while our democratic practices are part of the culture of the school," Kohn continues, "there is no formalized instruction for students regarding the rationale behind the principle." He hopes to use the First Amendment funding "to train staff and students in developing a curriculum that would enhance the culture and practices of the school."[25]

Academically, Quest pursues a personalized learning environment utilizing integrated curriculum and mastery learning. A student's experience at Quest begins with an application process and in-depth interview exploring what the school can provide the student and what the student wants from the school. Parents and students sign contracts agreeing to the school's rules and requirements.

The Quest curriculum is based on three sets of integrated standards: Academic Foundations; Essential Learner Behaviors; Workplace Tools. A strong effort is made to connect students to the local community and bring the community into the school through the service learning program. Consistent with the Humble Independent School Districts vision, the student and the school are seen as components of a larger community.

Assessment at Quest takes the form of evaluating students based on mastery of curriculum objectives and completion of a semester-long senior exhibition. This exhibition, presented to educators, students, parents, and community members, integrates public speaking, the use of technology and multimedia skills, and in-depth research concerning a modern-day social issue. To augment their research, students are required to create a social action plan that is implemented and sustainable.

---

[25] See www.firstamendmentschools.org/involve/highschool.aspx?item=quest, accessed July 28, 2005.

A site-based decision-making committee consisting of faculty, staff, students, parents and community members reviews the annual Campus Improvement Plan concerning programs and services. Additionally, the Quest advisory program, which they call families, has a representative assembly that provides for student input on policy, procedures and curriculum.

The school's straightforward mission statement[26] sums up all this work:

> Quest High School is committed to providing a personalized learning experience in a working partnership with the community to create life-long learners and successful members of society.

Educators working in an established school with longstanding (not to say entrenched) traditions may envy Quest's advantage as an intentionally created magnet school of choice. Nevertheless, the educational community undoubtedly benefits; in almost every aspect of its organization, programs, and practices, Quest High School offers solid models. In our common journey of reform efforts, it's great to have such a powerhouse in the wagon train.

Lanier High School: Aiming High in Jackson

Lanier High School is a public institution of slightly under 1000 students serving a predominately African American population in Jackson, Mississippi. The school aims to be among the very best high schools in the country and has already earned high praise, particularly in the areas of music and athletics. Since joining the First Amendment Schools network, the school seeks to become a model of democratic principles in action. The goal of training young people to lead the nation is an aspiration supported by a broad base of school stakeholders.

Among the many accomplishments thus far, Cecil Blue, a history teacher at Lanier, partnered with several students in producing an instructional video highlighting the First Amendment.

---

[26] See www.qhs.humble.k12.tx.us, accessed July 28, 2005.

The video, which includes case studies, has been made available to all Mississippi schools. Additionally, Lanier High School has restructured its student government, created a new school constitution, and inaugurated a new journalism program. The students have also been active in community politics, hosting local government meetings and presenting student issues to city officials and council members.

A school with rich traditions, it was named after William Henry Lanier, former president of Alcorn College, and first opened its doors in 1925. The school is proud to be home base for Dr. Robert Moses, founder of the Algebra Project. Lanier High School became a First Amendment Schools project school in 2002. School personnel have expressed high hopes for the First Amendment Schools initiative; according to teacher Ouida Atkins, "We believe that our revitalization of the school will spur the renewal of the community, which in turn will reinvigorate the school's well-being. Then, the school and the community will help to restore each other, and teach each other about the freedoms which make us all Americans—and which makes such renewal possible."[27]

The school's effort to become a laboratory of democracy extends to the homes of its students, as is evident in the excerpt on the following page from the school's First Amendment Newsletter:

Ten Ways Parents Can Reinforce
First Amendment Principles at Home

1. Learn the five freedoms guaranteed by the First Amendment.
2. Help your student complete his or her Student Citizenship Record.
3. Discuss current events that are affected by the First Amendment.
4. Discuss the idea that with every right comes responsibility. Discuss with your child what rights she/he has and what responsibilities come with those rights.

---

[27] See www.firstamendmentschools.org/involve/lanierhigh.html, accessed July 28, 2005.

5. Have a family vote to select dinner menus, books to read, family activities, etc. Discuss what happens after the choices are made.

6. When disagreements arise, encourage children to use persuasion instead of argument. Allow each person to voice his or her point of view and feelings without interruption.

7. Involve your children in community or family service projects.

8. Have children read a newspaper article with every fifth word blacked out. Then talk about censorship.

9. Read a book with your children about the Declaration of Independence and the Constitution, and/or the people who signed them.

10. Teach and model positive character traits.

http://www.jackson.k12.ms.us/school_sites/lanier/amend_news2.htm

The Lanier High School motto is *New Day, New Way, Restore the Legacy*. These seven words say a great deal about this school and its approach to improving the experiences of the students who attend Lanier. The school's three-year First Amendment Schools grant expired in June 2005; it now has the status of an alumni school. But it is unlikely that Lanier will lower its sights any time soon. The school has a strong tradition of success and an even stronger commitment to renewal. To quote the Lanier High School mission statement:

> Our mission is to provide students with a quality education that will allow them to become articulate in the spoken word, masterful in writing, and analytical in thought and function as a self-sufficient supporting adult.[28]

A worthy aim for the entire American educational system!

---

[28] See www.jackson.k12.ms.us/school_sites/lanier/index.htm, accessed July 28, 2005.

Butler Middle School: A Civic-Minded Middle School

For about five years, Butler Middle School has participated in the 3Rs (Rights, Responsibilities, and Respect) project, a statewide initiative in Utah and California that prepares educators to teach about religious liberty and religion in ways that are constitutionally permissible and educationally sound. The school has also belonged to the First Amendment Schools network since 2002. Young people in this school of 1,150 students in grades 7–9, located in Salt Lake City, Utah, benefit from two programs that promote democracy and individual freedoms.

As a result of seeing how the democratic process works, students at Butler are not timid about expressing their opinions. In fact the school has many programs that accentuate student voice and provide young people with a meaningful participation in school governance. In 2002, only 26 percent of the students at Butler agreed with the statement, "Students help make goals and rules at my school." Within a year, that figure ballooned to 69 percent, as the school established a student senate. Currently the Butler Student Senate is involved not only in developing rules and goals for the school, but also in problem solving and day-to-day decision-making.

One senate member wrote, "I do think that the senate really does work. It is a very good way for students to have a voice. A few examples are getting breakfast at the school (which I go to every day) and getting a tree in front of the school. (The tree was planted in honor of our men and women in the armed services in the war with Iraq.) Senate is not just a way to let the student body raise its voice, but it is also a way for the students to be updated every week about what is happening. I know my class appreciates knowing what is happening in the school. I think that having senators and giving suggestions is a good way to test our limits. Because we know our limits we can change what is within them."

The protocols for the Student Senate at Butler Middle School are steadily evolving. Students have worked to develop a senate application and formalize elections; they even wrote a senate oath to be taken during a citizenship assembly. As the students grow more skillful in the practice of democracy, adults have had to expand their view of student involvement. The typical adult response to student inquiries about district policy or state laws has been, "That is policy and we can't change that." Principal Beverly Ashby reports, "Adults in the school are starting to recognize that the senate is ready and capable of taking on issues beyond the walls of the school. We need to explain to them the steps necessary to pursue changing policy or law and see if they are committed enough to the issue and to the process to tackle it."

Many other developments at Butler Middle School demonstrate that schools can be places where students practice citizenship. The journalism program has grown in importance as students address issues that are important to them. Students have brought issues before the senate, such as bullying and the absence of clocks in the hallways, and achieved satisfactory resolutions. Within classrooms, teachers are providing students with more autonomy, stressing free expression, and honoring diversity. Many of the staff's professional development activities are related to the school's democratic initiatives.

All of these programs have served to create a school where students are truly experiencing the democratic process. In isolation, each of the initiatives would not be considered remarkable in a middle school setting, yet at Butler they are created under the backdrop of the guiding principles of the 3Rs and First Amendment Schools initiatives. Beverly Ashby, who has been the school's principal since the late 1990s, retired at the conclusion of the 2004–2005 school year, leaving a school that has made great strides in producing civic-minded graduates. In fact, the class of 2005 was the first group of students to have been involved in the First Amendment Schools project for their entire stay at Butler Middle School. As Ashby reflects, "We realize what great students and leaders they are, and we hope that they will continue to be involved in their schools and community." A fitting testimonial to the work of many at Butler Middle School—and a fitting challenge to schools throughout our nation.

Snapshots

This section offers snapshots of six schools that promote democratic experiences for their students and communities. Each of these six schools approaches the challenge of educating for citizenship from a slightly different angle; schools that decide to travel this road can choose from many paths. The information given here comes from the First Amendment Schools Web site,[29] which posts profiles of these and a host of other Project Schools and Affiliate Schools.

Park High School
Cottage Grove, Minnesota
Enrollment: 1,700, grades 9–12
http://www.sowashco.k12.mn.us/phs/index.asp

Cottage Grove lies about ten miles southeast of Saint Paul. Park High School's journalism program is reputed for its award-winning publications, including Minnesota's best yearbook award for 2004. The First Amendment Schools initiative forms the centerpiece of Park's celebration of student journalists, young citizens, and open and responsible expression. By teaching responsible journalism—including ethical and legal expectations—Park empowers students to perform with professional approaches. As Principal Walt Lyszak summarized, "We expect and trust the students to meet these expectations and, in fact, they do."

Cy-Fair High School
Cypress, Texas
Enrollment: 3,200, grades 9–12
http://schools.cfisd.net/cyfair/index.htm

Cy-Fair High School is the largest school affiliated with the First Amendment Schools network. Some thirty active organizations serve the school, the community, and beyond, including Model United Nations, Junior Achievement, Young Republicans and Young Democrats, Senior Men and Women, Civil Rights

---

[29] See www.firstamendmentschools.org, accessed July 28, 2005.

Club, Student Council, Key Club, and Amnesty International. During the 2004 election campaign, the school held a "Watch the Debate Night," and its Young Republicans and Democrats Clubs hosted their own debate. This high level of civic engagement creates a student body that cares about the future.

Ogden High School
Ogden, Utah
Enrollment: 1,672, Grades 9–12
http://www.ohs.ogden.k12.ut.us/

At Ogden High School, several strong programs involve a diverse population of students. The 100-member debate team has won seven state championships; a Youth Court hears cases involving student violations of school rules. Being a First Amendment Affiliate School has enriched the curriculum. "The entire staff teaches all students about the basic principles of the first amendment and how important they are to this country and each student's life," says teacher Mary Courney. "Educating students about citizenship is just as important to the school as academics."

Nogales High School
Nogales, Arizona
Enrollment: 1,750, Grades 9–12
http://www.nusd.k12.az.us/nhs/

Sitting directly on the Arizona and Mexico international border, Nogales High School has a student body of 98% Mexican-American ethnicity. The school's mission is to give all students the challenge, tools, and opportunity to exhibit learning. Nogales High School is a Senior Project School. The project consists of a research paper, a hands-on application of their learning, a portfolio that documents the application, and a speech to community members and teachers. The school seeks project topics that extend a greater awareness of the First Amendment to the community through individual action. Many students choose First Amendment or Bill of Rights related themes to exhibit their mastery of research, application, and speaking skills as required by the State of Arizona.

Johansen High School
Modesto, California
Enrollment: 2,968, grades 9–12
http://johansen.monet.k12.ca.us/

This large California high school was awarded a First Amendment Schools grant to develop a special First Amendment curriculum. The school conducted grade-level work days to align its social studies curriculum and strengthen its emphasis on the rights and responsibilities of the first amendment for all students. According to social studies department chair Ken Adair, "The collaboration with other government teachers focused our attention on the first amendment and helped us create continuity in what we teach in our department."

Cherry Hill High School West
Cherry Hill, New Jersey
Enrollment: 1625, grades 9–12
http://west.cherryhill.k12.nj.us/

One of three high schools in a growing district of 11,700 students, Cherry Hill High School West has been committed to character education since the late 1990s. In becoming a First Amendment Affiliate School, Cherry Hill West High School is now able to promote not only the respect and responsibility components of character education, but also the importance of character in American citizenship. Assistant Principal Allison Staffin states that "due to this involvement students have begun to take more interest in the political process. Students are really interested in what is going on, and having a specific role to play."

Conclusion:
Closing the Circle

We began our exploration of student voice with the idea of getting students to care—the assertion that unless we engage our students, not much else will matter. We examined the beliefs and attitudes that underpin schools where student voice makes a difference. We found that the educational practices that honor student voice also support student involvement and improve school climate. We delved into various programs that offer young people rich opportunities to grow as students and as citizens.

As our view widened, we found a wealth of inspirational models—schools that set high expectations for student engagement, schools where students rise to meet those expectations. We saw one example after another of students participating fully in their schools and in the wider community, practicing the skills so essential to civic engagement in a democratic society.

I'd like to close this journey with a brief excerpt from an editorial published in the January 27, 2005, issue of the Kennebunk High School newspaper, *Ramblings*.

Come on, KHS, get into it!

In the past couple of years, I have learned the importance of "caring." You'd be surprised at the magnitude of the results if you change your attitude toward school. You don't have to be a genius in any class. You don't necessarily have to understand the material the first, second or even third time it is taught, but if you actually care about learning it, you will learn it.

It is also important to care about yourself and other people. Everybody has talents and strengths that can pave the way to their future vocation. The harder you try and persevere, the farther you will go. Just think about that. A positive attitude can take you much farther than you think.

This student's heartfelt message holds the very essence of student voice. Not only does he get it, he is also encouraging others to find it. His school honors his voice; its newspaper respects his views. Something tells me that he will be a participant, a citizen, and a leader for life.

Bibliography

Alexander, Caroline (1998). *The Endurance: Shackleton's Legendary Antarctic Expedition*. New York: Alfred A. Knopf, Inc.

Armstrong, Lance (2001). *It's Not About the Bike*. New York: Berkley Publishing.

Beaudoin, Nelson (2005). *Stepping Outside Your Comfort Zone: Lessons for School Leaders*. Larchmont, New York: Eye on Education.

Benard, Bonnie (2004). *Resiliency: What We Have Learned*. Oakland, California: West Ed.

Littky, Dennis, with Samantha Grabelle (2004). *The Big Picture: Education Is Everyone's Business*. Alexandria, Virginia: Association for Supervision and Curriculum Development.

Littky, Dennis, and Samantha Grabelle (2004). Voting for homecoming queen does not prepare students for democracy. *Journal of the Coalition of Essential Schools* 21(1).

Prochaska, James O., Norcross, John C. and DiClemente, Carlo C. (1994). *Changing for Good: The Revolutionary Program That Explains the Six Stages of Change and Teaches You How to Free Yourself From Bad Habits*. New York: William Morrow and Company, Inc.

Rozycki, Edward G. (1999). Cloning student voice. First published in *Educational Horizons*, Summer 1997, 158-159.

Wigginton, Eliot (1986). *Sometimes a Shining Moment: The Foxfire Experience*. Garden City, New York: Anchor Books.